PROJECT MANAGEMENT STEP-BY-STEP

PROJECT MANAGEMENT STEP-BY-STEP

Larry Richman

AMACOM

American Management Association

New York • Atlanta • Brussels • Buenos Aires • Chicago • London • Mexico City
San Francisco • Shanghai • Tokyo • Toronto • Washington, D.C.

Special discounts on bulk quantities of AMACOM books are available to corporations, professional associations, and other organizations. For details, contact Special Sales Department, AMACOM, a division of American Management Association, 1601 Broadway, New York, NY 10019.
Tel.: 212-903-8316.   Fax: 212-903-8083.
Web site: www.amacombooks.org

This publication is designed to provide accurate and authoritative information in regard to the subject matter covered. It is sold with the understanding that the publisher is not engaged in rendering legal, accounting, or other professional service. If legal advice or other expert assistance is required, the services of a competent professional person should be sought.

"PMI" is a service and trademark of the Project Management Institute, Inc., which is registered in the United States and other nations. "PMP" is a certification mark of the Project Management Institute, Inc., which is registered in the United States and other nations. "PMBOK" is a trademark of the Project Management Institute, Inc., which is registered in the United States and other nations.

Library of Congress Cataloging-in-Publication Data

Richman, Larry.
      Project management step-by-step / Larry Richman.
        p. cm.
      Includes bibliographical references and index.
      ISBN 0-8144-7387-3
      1. Project management. I. Title.
    HD69.P75 R53 2002
    658.4'04—dc21

                         2002001987

Printing number

10   9   8   7   6   5   4   3   2   1

To my wife,
Teri,
for her patience during the thousands of hours in
writing, editing, and refining the book

CONTENTS

PREFACE

ORGANIZATION OF THIS BOOK

This book is divided into four sections. The first section describes the importance and function of project management. It defines the roles of the project managers, team members, clients, and customers. The second section teaches the skills and techniques of planning, estimating, budgeting, and scheduling a project. The third section describes how to execute a project, including controlling, reporting, and managing change and risk. The fourth section teaches the people skills needed to lead project teams.

HOW TO APPLY THIS BOOK TO REAL LIFE

To make this book more practical, consider a project you have recently worked on, or one you are currently working on, and keep it in mind as you read the book. Each chapter has application questions and exercises to help you consider how the concepts in the book apply to your real-life project. Several chapters also contain case studies that will help you understand and apply the issues to other projects.

The chapters in this book take you through the process of project management step-by-step. As you read each chapter, consider the tools, techniques, and processes you want to incorporate in your organization. Even if you intuitively already do many of the steps outlined in this book, you can increase your success at managing projects by setting up a process whereby everyone in your organization consistently uses these methods, tools, and techniques.

For the sake of simplicity in instruction, this book presents project management as a series of discrete steps performed in a defined sequence. In reality, these steps may be performed several times throughout the project. For example, some project planning steps may need to be repeated in various phases of project execution. Steps may also overlap and interact in various ways.

ADDITIONAL PROJECT MANAGEMENT INFORMATION

There are three Appendixes at the end of the book, which provide additional information and project management training. Appendix A contains suggested answers for the application exercises and case studies in the text. Appendix B is a glossary that defines all the project management terms used in this book. Appendix C provides suggested readings, resources, and Web sites, all of which are helpful sources of project management information.

The purchase of this book also grants you access to a special Internet site with additional resources to use with this book. Log on to the Project Management Center at *www.projectman.org* and access special areas of that site using the password *projectboy*.

ACKNOWLEDGMENT

I gratefully acknowledge the help of Gregg Johnson of the University of Phoenix for encouraging me to take on this project and for his review of the manuscript.

SECTION 1

PREPARING FOR PROJECT MANAGEMENT SUCCESS

SECTION OBJECTIVES

- Identify the differences between functional and project management.

- Understand trends in business management today and the need for project management.

- Identify the requirements of an effective project management system.

❖❖❖
CHAPTER 1

UNDERSTANDING THE IMPORTANCE OF PROJECT MANAGEMENT

Many people become project managers by accident. Someone assigns them to manage a project because of their areas of expertise, not because they have received any project management training. However, if you manage a project by accident, it will become a disaster!

Learning project management skills can help you complete projects on time, on budget, and on target. The discipline of project management includes proven strategies for clarifying project objectives, avoiding serious errors of omission, and eliminating costly mistakes. It also addresses the necessary people skills for getting the cooperation, support, and resources to get the job done.

Project management is not just for project managers. Team members need to know how carry out their parts of the project and business executives need to understand how to support project management efforts in the organization.

This chapter should help you understand what project management is and how projects are different from traditional functional work. It also explains why project management is necessary in today's business and non-profit organizations.

WHAT IS PROJECT MANAGEMENT?

Project management is a set of principles, methods, and techniques that people use to effectively plan and control project work. It establishes a sound basis for effective planning, scheduling, resourcing, decision-making, controlling, and replanning.

Project management principles and techniques help complete projects on schedule, within budget, and in full accordance with project specifications. At the same time, they help achieve the other goals of the organization, such as productivity, quality, and cost effectiveness.

The objective of project management is to optimize project cost, time, and quality.

THE HISTORY OF PROJECT MANAGEMENT

Project management has been around since the beginning of time. Noah was a project manager. It took careful planning and execution to construct the ark and gather two of every animal on earth, including all the necessary food and water. The pyramids of Egypt stand today because of thousands of projects and hundreds of project managers.

Although there have been brilliant project managers over the years, project management was not recognized as a formal management concept until operations research in the 1950s and 1960s pioneered methods and specialized tools to manage expensive, high-profile aerospace projects such as Polaris and Apollo. NASA and the U.S. Department of Defense established project management standards that they expected their contractors to follow. In the middle and late 1960s, business managers began searching for new techniques and organizational structures that would help them adapt quickly to changing environments. The 1970s and 1980s brought more published data on project management, leading to the development of theories, methods, and standards. The construction industry, for example, saw the potential benefits of formal project management and began to adopt standards and develop new techniques. Large-scale initiatives such as quality improvement and reengineering provided data, analysis, and problem solving techniques, but no structured discipline to implement them. Therefore, managers turned to project management for direction in implementing and tracking such large-scale projects.

By the 1990s, industries in both profit and nonprofit sectors came to realize that the size and complexity of their activities were unmanageable without adopting formal project management processes and tools.

PROJECT MANAGEMENT TODAY

Today, modern project management has emerged as a premier solution in business operations. Large and small organizations recognize that a structured approach to planning and controlling projects is a necessary core competency for success.

International organizations such as the Project Management Institute™ (PMI™) and the International Project Management Association (IPMA) promote project management by providing professional development programs. (See the "Suggested Resources" section in Appendix C at the end of this book for contact information on these and other organizations.) PMI offers Project Management Professional (PMP) certification to those who demonstrate competency in the field of project management through education and experience and by passing a rigorous certification exam. PMI sets standards and accredits degree-granting educational programs in project management. In 1987, PMI published the first *Project Management Body of Knowledge®* (*PMBOK®*) in an attempt to document and standardize generally accepted project management information and practices. The current edition, *A Guide to the Project Management Body of Knowledge*,[1] is a basic reference for anyone interested in project management. It provides a common lexicon and consistent structure for the field of project management.

Universities offer undergraduate and graduate degree programs in project management. Organizations such as PMI and ProjectWorld hold symposia and seminars throughout the year, which are great opportunities to increase basic skills, get new ideas by hearing current success stories, and network with other professionals. (See Appendix C at the end of this book for a list of organizations and Web sites.)

FUNCTIONAL WORK VERSUS PROJECT WORK

Project work and traditional functional work differ in significant ways, and it is important to understand these differences.

Functional Work

Functional work is routine, ongoing work. Each day, secretaries, financial analysts, and car salesmen perform functional work that is routine, even if their activities vary somewhat from day to day. A manager assigned to the specific function gives them training and supervision and manages them according to standards of productivity in terms of typing speed or sales quotas.

The following are distinguishing characteristics of functional work:

- Functional work is ongoing, routine work.

- Managers manage the specific function and provide technical direction.

- People and other resources are assigned to the functional department.

- Functional departments are responsible for the approved objectives of the function, such as technical competency, standards of performance and quality, and efficient use of resources.

Functional work is typically structured as a hierarchical organization with traditional formal lines of authority, as shown in Figure 1-1.

Project Work

In contrast to on-going, functional work, a project is "a temporary endeavor undertaken to create a unique product or ser-

Figure 1–1. Functional organizational structure.

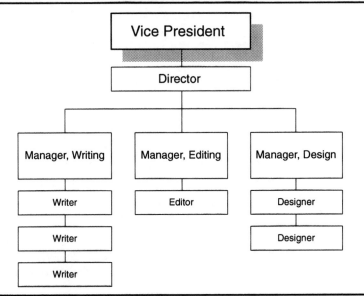

vice.''[2] Projects are *temporary* because they have a definite beginning and a definite end. They are *unique* because the product or service they create is different in some distinguishing way from similar products or services. The construction of a headquarters building for ABC Industries is an example of a project. The unique work is defined by the building plans and has a specific beginning and end. A project manager is responsible for the project, overseeing the contractors and managing the schedule and budget.

The following are distinguishing characteristics of project work:

- Project work is a unique, temporary endeavor.
- A project manager manages a specific project.
- People and other resources are not assigned to project managers on an ongoing basis, except for project management support.
- A project manager is responsible for the approved objectives of a project—such as budget, schedule, and specifications.

Project teams are typically not organized in the same hierarchical structure as that of typical functional groups. They are organized in one of various ways, which will be described in Chapter 2.

Figure 1-2 shows how functional and project responsibility fit together, using the functional departments in a publishing company, with project managers assigned to accomplish specific publication projects. Solid vertical lines show the functional responsibilities of the writing, editing, design, printing, and distribution departments. Broken horizontal lines show the project responsibilities of specific project managers assigned to given publications (projects). Since not all projects require the services of every functional department, circles indicate where people are assigned to a project. Project #2 uses outsourced

Figure 1–2. Responsibility grid.

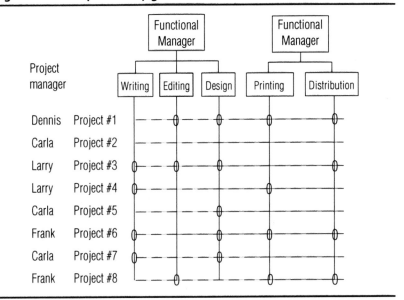

resources. Project #3 is a video that uses an external video duplication company rather than the internal printing facility.

A project manager manages horizontally via projects rather than vertically via functional experts. Figure 1-2 shows that Dennis is responsible for project #1. To get the job done, he must enlist the help of editors and designers from one functional manager and printers and distributors from another functional manager. In some organizations, functional managers are called *resource managers* because they are responsible for assigning resources to the project.

In the real world, there might be an overlap between project and functional managers. If functional resources (other than a project management staff) are assigned to a project manager, then that manager has functional responsibility and is acting as both project manager and functional manager. If projects are assigned to a functional manager, then that manager also has project responsibility and is acting in both roles. Figure 1-3 compares functional and project work.

Figure 1-3. Comparison of project and functional work.

	Functional	*Project*
Type of work	Repeated, on-going.	Unique, no rehearsal. Often involves change.
Focus	Operations, accomplishing effective work.	Completing the project.
Management responsibility	Managing people.	Managing work.
Budgets	On-going operational budgets.	Project budgets to fund specific projects.
Responsiveness to customers and changing environments	Less responsive. Longer response time.	More responsive. Shorter response time.
Consistency and standards	Industry standards.	May have few standards because work is unique.
Cross-cultural relevance	Varies across cultures.	More constant across cultures.
Risk	On-going work is stable and less risky.	Higher risk because work is unique and unknown.
Visibility	May have little visibility if standards are not met.	Obviously noted when project objectives are not met.

The traditional functional approach is not adequate in a project environment and does not promote quality work on time and within budget. The project approach promotes the innovation, experimentation, and entrepreneurship needed in the world today.

WHY PROJECT MANAGEMENT IS NECESSARY IN TODAY'S WORLD

The need for project management is becoming increasingly apparent in the world today. Speed, quality, and cost control are taking on increased significance in business, government, and nonprofit sectors. Project management allows managers to plan and manage strategic initiatives that generate new revenue in expanding sectors of the market. Project management tools decrease time to market, control expenses, ensure quality products, and enhance profitability. Project management helps to sell products and services by positively differentiating them from their competitors. Project management is one of the most important management techniques for ensuring the success of an organization.

The global marketplace and e-commerce are forcing organizations to change. Consider the business trends in the next section.

Today's Business Trends

- The focus is on high-quality, speed-to-market, and superior customer satisfaction. This can be accomplished only across functional lines of authority in a project environment. With the shift from mass production to custom production of goods and services, project management is an increasingly important aspect of a responsive management style. Businesses are shifting from traditional hierarchical management to project management. Organizational charts are changing from vertical structures to team-centered project structures.

- The traditional job of doing the same tasks every day is disappearing as routine office and factory work become automated. Middle management is also disappearing as companies rely on computers to gather and analyze information. The new focus is on projects and project teams assigned to solve specific problems. Teams might be set up to design a new product or re-engineer the ordering process. Projects are conceived, staffed up, completed, then shut down. Project teams come and go with problems and opportunities.

- The traditional career path is changing. Companies offer less job security as they refocus on core competencies and outsource noncore work. They teach marketable skills but don't promise a job tomorrow. People define their careers less by companies ("I work for Microsoft") and more by professions ("I design computer programs"). Personal success is measured by the value of the projects on which a person works. The goal is growth in the profession, not movement up the corporate ladder into management. Pay is determined by skill level and the marketability of the person's services rather than by managerial hierarchy.

■ The typical company of tomorrow has four basic careers, as illustrated in Figure 1-4. This has been the norm for decades in Hollywood, where casting agents match actors with projects. In the entertainment industry, producers are the top-level management, casting and talent agents are the resource providers, movie directors are the project managers, and actors and crew are the talent.

A Proactive Management Style

Today's trends mean that management expects more with less. There is more pressure with less time, more work with less staff,

Figure 1-4. Careers in the typical company of tomorrow.

Career	Title	Function
Top-level management	CEO, president, executive VP	Sets strategy.
Resource provider	CFO, CIO, HR manager, VP of marketing, engineering, etc.	Provides budget; develops and manages expert staffs.
Project manager	Project manager	Uses money and people from the resource providers.
Talent	chemist, engineer, accountant, programmer	Reports to resource provider but spends much time on project teams.

and more cost control with less tolerance for mistakes. The solution to this dilemma lies in a proactive rather than reactive management style. Systematic project management is a proactive style. Figure 1-5 shows a comparison of reactive and proactive styles.

Many companies conduct business by means of projects. Each project is justified because it creates a product or service that the company can sell or because it reduces or controls costs. As the number of a company's potential projects increases, there is an increased necessity to choose the right projects and execute them more efficiently. As competition between vendors increases, the winning company will be the one with superior project management processes, reports, tools, and organization.

Organizations that were once hierarchical and bureaucratic now realize that success requires internal and external networking. Functional departments are no longer self-sufficient, but interdependent. Teams are formed from various functional departments to accomplish project work. When one project is completed, individuals are regrouped into another team to take on yet another project.

Figure 1-5. Comparison of reactive and proactive management styles.

Reactive	Proactive
Fire fighting.	Planning and control.
Managing by instinct gut feel notes on a napkin.	Managing by information analysis control system.
Speaking in generalizations.	Using charts and graphs.
Not seeing the big picture.	Seeing the big picture.
Not planning because it is a waste of time. Not anticipating changes.	Planning thoroughly on the front end with contingency plans for potential problems.

DEFINITIONS

Functional manager. A person assigned to manage a specific function (such as accounting, manufacturing, or marketing) and to provide technical direction. Also called a *resource manager.*

Project. "A temporary endeavor undertaken to create a unique product or service." A project has a definite beginning and end.[3]

Project management. A set of principles, methods, and techniques used to plan and control project work effectively.

Project manager. The person who manages a specific project, who is expected to meet the approved objectives of the project, including project scope, budget, and schedule.

APPLICATION QUESTIONS

1. How could you benefit from using more project management principles?

2. Does your organization understand the difference between project and functional work? How can you help co-workers and management implement project management philosophies?

3. Why is project management a sound strategy in today's business world?

APPLICATION EXERCISES

1. Draw a responsibility grid for your organization and define project and functional responsibility.

2. List problems you currently experience in managing projects. As you read subsequent chapters, identify ways in which you can address these problems.

NOTES

1. Project Management Institute, *A Guide to the Project Management Body of Knowledge (PMBOK® Guide)*, 2000, p. 4.
2. Ibid.
3. Ibid.

❖❖❖
CHAPTER 2

ORGANIZING FOR PROJECT MANAGEMENT EFFICIENCY

Many organizations have no formal project management structure. When a project is conceived, management might appoint a project manager and team members with little attention to the skills needed for the job. They take people from their regular jobs to work on the project—or worse yet, they ask team members to do the project in addition to their regular work.

This chapter discusses the need for the organization to formally adopt project management methodologies. It presents the major organizational structures and discusses the advantages and disadvantages of each. Finally, it gives some considerations on how to organize for greater efficiency and continuity in projects.

ADOPTING A PROJECT MANAGEMENT PHILOSOPHY

People throughout the organization must understand and implement common project management principles. Everyone must recognize project management as a professional discipline with specific skills and tools.

Senior management must recognize the need for project management and be willing to establish a formal project management system. Managing projects is considerably different from managing functional groups. Senior executives need to recognize that project management requires special concepts, skills, and tools. Managers schooled in traditional concepts of business management might find this difficult to understand. Functional line managers might have difficulty understanding the difference between functional and project responsibilities.

Implementing a project management system requires more than lip service; senior management must provide the time, budget, and resources to do it. The entire organization must have a long-term commitment to the project management process and support it without constantly shifting priorities.

The role and authority of the project managers must be clearly defined and supported. Project managers are not simply people selected from among the project teams; they need to have project management skills. If management simply assigns a technical person to be the project manager, the organization loses in two ways. First, if the person does not also have project management skills, the project might fail. Second, the organization loses a good technical person from the project team.

The organization also must be willing to change. Functional departments with a strong sense of uniqueness might feel that project managers cannot fully understand or correct their problems. Functional managers who have been unable to solve problems might work against the project manager's success. In some cases, people resist the project manager's tools (such as network planning and computerized tracking) because they represent change. Change is often painful and takes time.

Your project management system needs to be adapted to your organization's specific corporate culture and needs. No one system works equally well in all organizations. Be willing to adapt the system as you experience successes or failures so the system can operate a optimum efficiency in your organization.

For project management to be effective in any organization, there should be formal, written policies and procedures that explain the role and authority of project managers and how project management functions in the organization. Figure 2-1 is an example of such a written policy statement.

ORGANIZATIONAL STRUCTURES

The organizational structure strongly influences how efficiently project management operates. It often constrains the availability of resources or the terms under which resources are available to the project. Organizational structures typically span the spectrum from functional to project, with a variety of matrix structures in between, as will be discussed below. Any of these variations might be appropriate and effective if the advantages and disadvantages are understood and handled properly. The next sections cover characteristics, advantages, and disadvantages of functional, project, and matrix organizational structures.

Functional

The classic functional organization is a hierarchy in which people are grouped into functional divisions, such as marketing or production. Each employee has one clear superior. In functional organizations, the scope of projects is typically limited to the boundaries of the functional division. Each division has its own

Figure 2-1. Example of a project management policy statement.

Project Management Division
Subject: Project Management System   Policy 5
Date of Origin: 15 April 2003   Revised 16 May 2004

Policy

The company manages projects according to the project management system outlined in this policy.

Definition of a project

A temporary endeavor undertaken to create a unique product or service.

Responsibility

The director of the Project Management Division is responsible for the operation of the project management system. The director prepares policy statements and maintains the policy and procedure manual. The director tracks all approved projects and reports project status to senior management.

Project objectives

All projects are defined in terms of (1) cost, (2) time, and (3) project scope. These objectives are the basis for project approval, budgeting, tracking, and reporting.

Project managers

A project manager is assigned to each project when it is approved. The manager may be from the Project Management Division or from another functional division as needed. The project manager is responsible to see that the project accomplishes its objectives of cost, time, and project scope. The lines of responsibility and communication with senior management will be identified as needed with each project.

project managers who report to the head of the division, as illustrated in Figure 2-2. These project managers operate independently from project managers in other divisions.

Characteristics

■ Project managers operate within the division and have a level of expertise within their areas of responsibility. For example,

Figure 2-2. Functional organizational structure.

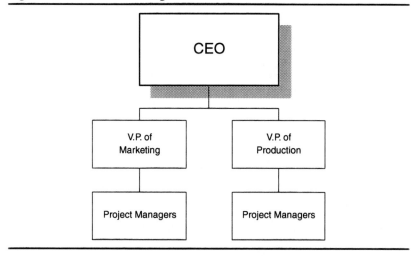

project managers in the marketing division come from the ranks of salespeople and have a level of knowledge or experience in sales.

■ Directors of the functional divisions manage both project and functional personnel. They are responsible for defining requirements, scheduling work, setting priorities, providing facilities, acquiring and managing resources, adhering to company policies, and ensuring quality.

■ People are assigned to work on projects for which their skills and services are needed. They might be moved around within the division wherever they are needed.

Advantages

■ Projects can be completed more accurately. Because project managers and team members have expertise in the functional area, project requirements can be defined and challenged intelligently. This means that fewer changes will be made during the life of a project and that a more practical end product can result.

■ Project personnel are accountable for their work and must accept success or failure. Since they must live with the end result of the project, they are committed to it.

■ Because personnel have functional expertise, learning time is reduced and projects can be completed quickly. Problem situations can be identified and corrected quickly.

Disadvantages

■ The focus on the needs of the functional division might make it difficult to see and respond to the needs of the organization as a whole. Enterprise policies and practices might not be enforced uniformly across divisions.

■ Project control and status reporting to upper management is not standardized across the organization. It might be difficult for senior executives to manage the various projects within the organization.

■ Project costs tend to have little or no accounting. Many aspects of a project are handled as ongoing functional work of the division, so it might be difficult to identify and account for the true cost of a project.

■ The distinction between project and functional roles might be vague and projects might be lost in routine work.

Project

In a project organization, projects are centralized in a separate division of skilled project managers that serves the project management needs of all divisions of the company (See Figure 2-3). This is often referred to as a *project office* and is becoming increasingly popular in organizations.

Characteristics

■ A central group is responsible for planning, controlling, managing, and reporting the progress of all projects in the organization.

Figure 2-3. Project organizational structure.

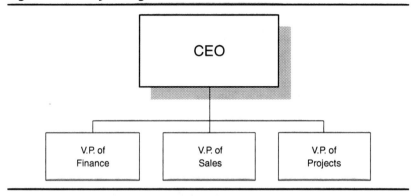

- Project managers have a great deal of independence and authority.

- Team members can be colocated.

Advantages

- A formal project management system is adopted and applied uniformly throughout the organization. This common understanding and application of project management practices typically creates high efficiency in the organization. Projects are more often completed on time, within budget, and in accordance with project scope.

- Common standards of planning, controlling, and reporting exist throughout the life of each project and are applied across all projects. These common standards aid communication and provide efficiency.

- Highly-skilled project managers can be available for the benefit of all. Costs can be reduced by using common tools (such as project management software) to manage all projects.

- Centralized data from all projects can be analyzed and applied to future projects to improve the accuracy of estimates and practices. A centralized organizational structure makes it easier to see productivity trends and take steps to improve processes in the organization.

- All projects of the organization can be managed as a whole. Enterprise portfolio management allows senior management to set priorities across projects and allocate resources for the overall good of the organization.

Disadvantages

- Standards and documentation can become excessive, and without careful vigilance, this centralization of project managers and practices can become self-serving. Rather than serving the needs of the project office, careful focus must be given to the needs of the project and the people it benefits.

- If processes become excessive, the total cost to manage a project under a centralized organizational structure can be higher than under other structures. The project office must constantly assess the value they provide to ensure that the value exceeds cost.

- Qualified technical leaders might be scarce. Project managers might not have the technical background needed for a project, and might have little access to people with the appropriate knowledge and skills.

- Project managers might seem unresponsive to the needs of people who request their time and skills. Because project managers are located in a separate project office, they might become out of touch with the needs and practices of individual departments.

Matrix

Matrix organizations are a blend of functional and project organizations. A weak matrix organization (see Figure 2-4) has many of the characteristics of a functional organization, and the project manager role is more that of a coordinator or expediter with

Figure 2–4. Weak matrix organization.

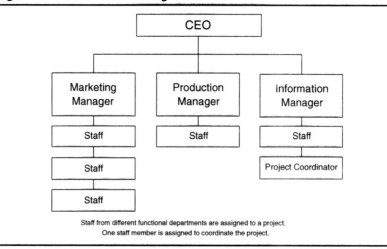

Staff from different functional departments are assigned to a project.
One staff member is assigned to coordinate the project.

limited authority. A strong matrix organization (see Figure 2-5) has many of the characteristics of a project organization, with a full-time project manager who has significant authority and a project administrative staff. In a matrix organization, the project team has a dual reporting role to a project manager, coordinator,

Figure 2–5. Strong matrix organization.

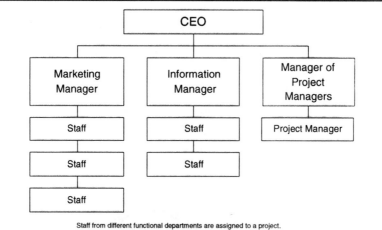

Staff from different functional departments are assigned to a project.
Project Manager is assigned to the project.

or expediter (who provides project management skills) and a functional manager (who provides technical and functional skills).

Characteristics

■ Because a matrix organization has characteristics of both the project and functional organizations, project personnel report both to functional and project lines.

■ Project personnel report to a functional manager for definition of requirements, feasibility and economic evaluation, changes in priorities, allocation of work, and ultimate success or failure in meeting their goals.

■ Project personnel report to a project manager for refining tasks and assignments, planning and budgets, and project schedules.

In a strong matrix organizational structure, the project manager has more power than the functional manager. In a weak matrix structure, the balance of power leans toward the functional manager.

Advantages

■ A matrix structure capitalizes on the advantages of both a project structure (project office) and a functional structure. Personnel and skills are less redundant, and when expertise is scarce, it can be applied more flexibly and efficiently to different projects.

■ The focus on teamwork easily accommodates changes in personnel requirements. Conflicts between project requirements and functional organization policies are perceived and resolved more readily.

■ The expertise of both project and functional management is available to assist in the project, and both can be applied to handle complex issues and coordinate various tasks.

■ This can often result in completing the project in less time and at lower cost.

Disadvantages

■ Dual management lines make communications more difficult to manage. When team members receive conflicting instructions from project and functional managers, time and effort are wasted clarifying the communication. The team might be unable to react fast enough to meet changing project requirements.

■ Conflicts and competition can exist between project and functional management. In the process of resolving conflicting priorities, project personnel can become confused and demoralized.

■ If conflicting priorities and personal power struggles are not quickly resolved, it can be damaging—or fatal—to the project.

Projects are influenced by the organizational structure under which they operate. The chart in Figure 2-6 shows the project manager authority in each of the organizational types.

FUNCTIONING EFFECTIVELY

Now that you understand the basic organizational structures, compare them with your organization and identify your current structure. Reread the advantages and disadvantages of your organizational structure and keep them in mind as you operate within that structure.

When faced with difficulties, many project managers jump to the conclusion that restructuring the organization will solve all the problems. Although it is important to have the right organizational structure, it is unhealthy to reorganize too often.

Figure 2-6. Project manager authority by organizational type.

Organiza-tional structure	Project manager authority	Percent of personnel assigned full-time to project work	Project manager's role	Common titles for project manager	Project manage-ment staff
Functional	Little or none	None	Part-time	Project Facilitator or Coordi-nator	Part-time
Weak matrix	Limited	0–25%	Part-time	Project Coordi-nator or Leader	Part-time
Balanced matrix	Low	15–60%	Part-time or full-time	Project Coordi-nator or Manager	Part-time
Strong matrix	Moderate	50–95%	Full-time	Project or Program Manager	Full-time
Project	High to almost total	85–100%	Full-time	Project or Program Manager	Full-time

Petronius Arbiter already illustrated this fallacy about two-thousand years ago:

> We trained hard, but it seemed that every time we were beginning to form up into teams we would be reorganized. I was to learn later in life that we tend to meet any new situation by reorganizing, and a wonderful method it can be for producing the illusion of progress while creating confusion, inefficiency, and demoralization.[1]

As you have seen, each possible organizational structure has both advantages and disadvantages. Before you reorganize, be sure that the advantages outweigh the disadvantages to your organization. The advantages must also be significant enough to make up for the confusion and pain of making the change. Reorganizing has a significant impact on any organization. Don't underestimate the lost productivity during the time it takes to make the change. It will take time for people to begin to function efficiently under the new structure.

DEFINITIONS

Enterprise portfolio management. Managing all projects of the organization as a whole by setting priorities and allocating resources across projects.

Functional organization. A hierarchical organizational structure in which each functional division has its own project managers who operate independently from project managers in other divisions.

Matrix organizational structure. An organizational structure that is a blend of functional and project structures. The project team reports both to a project manager (who provides project management skills) and a functional manager (who provides specific job-related skills).

Project organization. An organizational structure in which an autonomous division of project managers is responsible for planning, controlling, managing, and reporting the progress of all projects in the organization.

APPLICATION EXERCISES

1. Determine which of the basic organizational types describes your current organization. Draw a chart of your current organizational structure, using solid lines to show formal reporting relationships and broken lines to show lines of communication.

2. Review the characteristics, advantages, and disadvantages listed in this chapter for your organizational type. List the things you need to do to work effectively within this structure.

APPLICATION QUESTIONS

1. Is your current organizational structure the most appropriate, given the culture and current needs of your organization? Why or why not?

2. What other organizational type might be appropriate for your organization? Considering the relative advantages and disadvantages of the current and alternative structures, what additional value would the alternative structure provide?

3. What is the current level of implementation of project management in your organization?

4. What can you do to better implement project management?

NOTE

1. Quoted in Robert Townsend, *Up the Organization* (New York: Alfred A. Knopf, 1970), p. 162. Robert Townsend lists the date as "circa AD 60."

❖❖❖
CHAPTER

3

DEFINING THE ROLES OF THE PROJECT MANAGER AND THE TEAM

The role of the project manager can be a tricky one, especially when the project manager has no formal authority over the people he or she must work with to get the job done. This chapter defines the roles of the project manager and the project team members. It defines the skills of a project manager and discusses the balance needed in responsibility, accountability, and authority.

THE ROLE OF THE PROJECT MANAGER

The project manager is the person assigned to manage a specific project and is expected to meet the approved objectives of a project, including project scope, budget, and schedule. The project manager leads the project and provides vision, direction, and encouragement. The project manager's job is to ensure that the project is realistic, necessary, and well defined. The project manager takes the lead in project planning to determine the schedules, resource plans, and budgets necessary to accomplish the project objectives. Once the project plan has been approved by top management, the project manager carries out the plan. This includes carefully monitoring and reporting on progress, resolving problems as they arise, controlling any changes in the project plan, and managing risk. When all project objectives have been met, the project manager declares the project completed.

The project manager has overall responsibility for planning, organizing, integrating, controlling, leading, decision-making, communicating, and building a supportive climate for the project.

Except for a project management support team, people and other resources are not typically assigned directly to project managers. In a large project, the project manager might have a staff of clerks, accountants, and other people to help with the numerous responsibilities involved in managing the project. In a small project, there might be no support team.

PROJECT MANAGER SKILLS

Figure 3-1 shows the basic skills a project manager needs. A project manager needs to be strong in all five areas to be successful.

Project Management Skills

Project management skills include the tools of the trade to plan and execute a project, such as being able to estimate costs and prepare workable schedules and adequate budget plans. To exe-

Figure 3-1. Basic project manager skills.

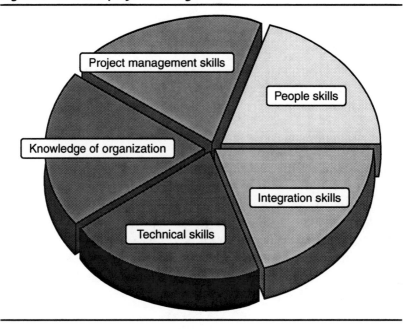

cute a project, a project manager needs to be able to analyze status information, prepare clear reports, and conduct project audits. These technical skills are discussed later in this book, in Sections 2 and 3. To be successful, a project manager should constantly improve skills in these areas through reading books and attending seminars and workshops. Universities, private training companies, and organizations such as the Project Management Institute routinely offer training opportunities. (See Appendix C at the end of this book for a list of organizations that provide training.)

People Skills

In working with team members, project managers use a combination of formal authority and persuasion skill. Authority is the ability to require another person to accept responsibility to produce a desired result. Persuasion is the ability to convince another person to accept such responsibility. The stronger a project manager's people skills, the greater the chance of successfully leading the project team. The project manager needs to be a master at communication and have the skills to manage conflict and change. (See Chapters 24, 25, and 29 for a discussion of these skills.)

Integration Skills

One of the project manager's primary duties is to be sure that the many elements of the project are properly coordinated. In particular, the various phases of project work such as planning, execution, reporting, and control must be integrated. The more complex the product, the more integration is needed. For example, the project manager might have to integrate electrical drawings from the engineering staff with functional specifications from the civil engineers. Engineers and designers should be involved not only in the design process, but also in the approval of the final design and specifications. Other players that likely need to be involved in the approval and acceptance phases include accounting and executive management to sign off on the project.

Project integration management also involves making trade-offs among competing options to accomplish the project objectives.

Technical Skills

Since project managers do not do the actual work of the project, they do not need the same technical skill level as the people performing the work. However, the more expertise the project manager has in the technical area of the project, the greater his effectiveness in managing the project. As the project manager integrates all aspects of the project, technical expertise is essential to identify potential problems.

However, as the project manager gains technical experience, she must also be careful to maintain a broad perspective and not let technical expertise lead to micro-managing—or worse yet, doing—the project work! She must concentrate on managing the project, allowing team members to perform the technical work and confining her technical involvement to evaluating the work of the team.

Knowledge of the Organization

The most proficient project management skills in the world will not compensate for a procedural blunder caused by not understanding the company culture, policies, personalities, or politics. The project manager negotiates with many people and needs to know their personalities, needs, and desires. The more he knows about the organization, the better equipped that manager is to maneuver around pitfalls and get what is needed for the project. Every organization has a unique culture and individual divisions within an organization often have their own personalities. Understanding these cultures and personalities can help a project manager be more successful.

THE MAKEUP OF A PROJECT MANAGER

Project management is a combination of many ingredients. Among these are large measures of common sense, ambition, flexibility, resourcefulness, and a healthy appetite for negotiation, and a genuine belief that the service performed is of value to the organization.

An effective project manager involves many people in the planning process and asks many questions: "What could go wrong?" "What if this happens?" The project manager anticipates problems and disagreements and builds agreements out of these conflicts. She takes every opportunity to build commitment from the various members of the project team, and she keeps appropriate people informed and involved throughout the process, soliciting input and suggestions.

No matter how well a project manager plans and executes a project, there will always be problems. The creative challenge is to be able to use imagination and experience to solve the problems in creative ways. The problems that arise are seldom unique. Successful project managers solve problems by applying their cumulative knowledge and experience to each obstacle. Over time, their realm of experience likely offers a precedent to almost any problem. Lessons learned in dealing with one project can, if applied imaginatively, go a long way toward solving similar problems in other projects.

However, experience alone is not enough to make an individual a successful project manager. Experience without the imagination to use it constructively and creatively is more likely to be a handicap than an advantage. For some people, years of experience serve as a straitjacket. They are blinded by their past experience and can only repeat what they first learned. They can't imagine new ways of addressing problems. Instead of adapting what they know to new situations, they try to make all new situations conform to patterns with which they are familiar.

The successful project manager is both a specialist and a generalist. As a generalist, the manager has broad technical knowledge of the diverse factors that affect a project, including aspects of the organization's operation and the related industry. As a specialist, the manager has a depth of technical knowledge about the project at hand. He succeeds because of a drive to understand the requirements, operations, and problems of clients, the project team, and the industry in general.

A good example of the importance of gaining both specific and general knowledge is found in the book *How to Be a Successful*

Executive,[1] where J. Paul Getty tells of a company that was embarking on an extensive plant modernization and expansion program. Just before the company placed an order for very expensive production machinery, one of the company's junior executives learned of an obscure company that had developed vastly improved machinery. The company was saved from making a huge investment in machinery that would have soon been obsolete, and instead obtained the latest equipment well ahead of its competitors.

This is a good example of an individual's alertness and enterprise, but it is not the full story. The junior executive was not a technical expert or engineer. His duties were concerned with sales, not production. After a meeting at which the plant modernization program was discussed, he took the initiative to research information about the new machinery in an obscure trade journal. His keen interest helped the company succeed.

A project manager who shows this type of initiative and understanding can have positive impact on the cost, quality, and timeliness of projects.

PROJECT MANAGER RELATIONSHIPS AND TOOLS

The skills you use as a project manager vary depending on your relationship with others. You might be more effective as a leader, negotiator, salesperson, or broker of information and services, depending on whom you are dealing with and the nature of your relationship with them, as illustrated in Figure 3-2.

RESPONSIBILITY, ACCOUNTABILITY, AND AUTHORITY

A common cause of problems in managing projects is a breakdown in the balance of responsibility, accountability, and au-

Figure 3-2. Project manager relationships and tools.

Relationship	Your role	Negotiating tools
Subordinate (people who report directly to you, team members, or vendors) You rely on them for results. They rely on you for performance reviews and payment.	Leader	Formal, written objectives Performance management (feedback, consequences)
Peer (support groups, team members, functional managers) You rely on them for results. They do not rely on you for performance reviews or payment.	Negotiator, salesperson or broker	Informal goals Performance management Performance contract (when necessary)
Superior (your boss, senior management, client, or customers) You rely on them to define the project and to provide resources, your performance review, and payment. They rely on you for results.	Salesperson and broker	Technical analysis and information Alternatives and recommendations Sales presentation

thority. Therefore, it is important that the project manager understands these issues and how to keep them in balance, because they can have a dramatic effect on how effectively she executes the management role. Figure 3-3 illustrates the relationship among these three management aspects.

Responsibility

Responsibility is an agreement between two or more people for the purpose of achieving a desired result. A project manager is responsible for accomplishing the project; however, the manager

Figure 3-3. The relationship of responsibility, authority, and accountability.

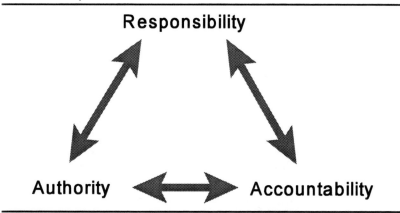

might assign all or part of that responsibility to other people on the team. It is important to remember, though, that even when the manager has passed along all or part of the responsibility for completing tasks associated with the project, the project manager still retains *full* responsibility for the final result. The project manager must be sure the assigned responsibility is clearly stated and the expected results are mutually understood and accepted by all parties.

Accountability

Accountability is a consequence of assigned responsibility. When a project manager assigns responsibility to another person, the manager must hold that person accountable for achieving the desired result. The accountability must be consistent with the responsibility assigned. For example, if a manager assigns a contractor to remodel an office, the manager should hold the contractor accountable for the responsibility assigned. This may include quality of work performed, adherence to schedule, and completing the job within budget. However, the manager should not hold the contractor responsible for lost productivity when workers moved to a temporary office before the remodeling began, because this was out of the control of the contractor and not part of the responsibility of the remodeling job. Although such inconsistent accountability is clearly unreasonable, it often happens.

Accountability is a major source of information and motivation. A reliable system of accountability makes good performance visible and provides a basis for accurate performance appraisals. It shows team members that good performance matters and is rewarded. When a project manager holds team members accountable, it helps to identify and focus on the sources of problems. Accountability helps decrease poor performance and increase good performance.

Authority

Authority is the power given to a person to complete the assigned responsibility. It includes the appropriate access to resources to complete the job, such as access to personnel or signature authority for the expenditure of funds. Authority must be commensurate with the responsibility assigned and appropriate to the accountability. To continue with our previous example of the office remodeling job, the manager should give the contractor the appropriate authority to complete the work. This may include a budget and access to the building commensurate with the size and scope of the remodeling job. A budget of $25,000 for a job estimated at $50,000 would not grant the contractor the authority, or power, to complete the job. If the schedule requires overtime and night work, the manager needs to grant workers 24-hour access to the building. If he does not, he should not hold the contractor accountable if the job runs over schedule.

If a person has little experience or skill in a particular area, the project manager might need to give authority in increments and do more checking up at the beginning. Then, as skill level and experience increase, the manager can grant more authority and check up less often, until full authority is warranted.

Maintaining the Balance

Project managers must maintain good balance in assigning responsibility, delegating authority, and holding people accountable. The authority must be appropriate for the responsibility and the accountability must be commensurate with the authority and the responsibility.

Successful organizations have written policies and procedures that define how responsibility, accountability, and authority work in the project management environment. It is important to define in writing the specific responsibilities and authority the project manager will have in terms of personnel, equipment, materials, and funds. Will the project manager have authority to hire and terminate team members or will the functional managers handle these responsibilities? What purchase authority will the project manager have over equipment and materials necessary to the project? What signature authority will the project manager have over other project expenditures?

ROLE OF TEAM MEMBERS

Team members are the people who work with the project manager directly or indirectly to accomplish project goals and complete project activities. Team members can have various roles in the project, such as engineers, technicians, construction workers, and others needed to perform the project work. Each project is unique, and so are the roles of the people performing the work.

In each project, it is important to identify all the players and define their roles and responsibilities. An information technology project, for example, might include the roles shown in Figure 3-4. It only takes a short while and pays great dividends throughout the life of the project as individual understands their roles and how to interface with other team members. When it does not happen, communications are often confused or misdirected and conflicts and power struggles arise.

DEFINITIONS

Integration management. The processes required to ensure that the various elements of the project are properly coordinated.

Project manager. The person assigned to manage a specific project, who is expected to meet the approved objectives of the project, including project scope, budget, and schedule.

Team members. The people who work with the project manager directly or indirectly to accomplish project goals and complete project activities.

APPLICATION EXERCISE

1. List five factors that inhibit your success in managing projects. Prioritize them in order of their importance to you (with number 1 being the most important).

2. Rank each factor on your ability to change it (with number 1 being the most open to change). Plot the factors on the grid in Figure 3-5. Locate the Priority ranking along the left side and the Ability to Change across the bottom. Place the letter of the factor (A–E) in the grid where the two coordinates meet.

The chart in Figure 3-6 rates the items as they fall into the four quadrants. Focus first on issues with high priority and high ability to change. These are the issues that are most important, and deserve your attention. Bring to the attention of management those with high priority and low ability to change so they can determine how these issues can be addressed.

Figure 3-4. Typical management roles and responsibilities in an information technology project.

Role	Responsibilities
Product Manager	■ Represents the needs of customers and stakeholders ■ Defines business requirements ■ Manages customer expectations ■ Manages the product launch
Project Manager	■ Manages systems planning and analysis ■ Prepares the functional specification document ■ Identifies and procures resources ■ Manages the master schedule ■ Coordinates team ■ Reports status
Development Manager	■ Performs system design ■ Writes reliable code ■ Maintains development schedule
Test/QA Manager	■ Owns the quality of the product ■ Participates in code review ■ Performs integration testing (migration and process) ■ Tracks bugs and issues
User Education Manager	■ Writes online help and user documentation ■ Participates in usability testing ■ Prepares and delivers the training
Logistics Planner	■ Plans the alpha and beta roll-out ■ Coordinates with help desk and IT Operations ■ Plans the installation of hardware and software ■ Provides support and troubleshooting ■ Creates a disaster recovery plan
Systems Architect	■ Assists in definition of business requirements ■ Provides project design assistance ■ Defines product technical and location architectures ■ Ensures architecture issues and questions are resolved
Executive Committee	■ Provides executive direction and issue resolution ■ Ensures stakeholder views are represented ■ Encourages compliance with company IT architecture ■ Ensures operability and integration between departments ■ Obtains funding

Figure 3–5. Grid for rating issues inhibiting success in managing projects.

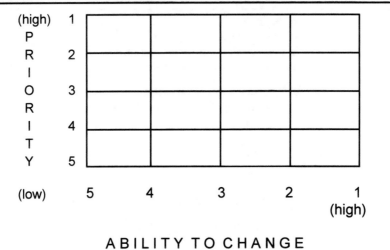

Figure 3–6. Chart for rating issues inhibiting success in managing projects.

(high) 1			
P	High Priority; Low Ability to Change		High Priority; High Ability to Change
R 2			
I			
O 3			
R			
I 4	Low Priority; Low Ability to Change		Low Priority; High Ability to Change
T			
Y 5			
(low)	5 4	3	2 1 (high)

ABILITY TO CHANGE

Focus next on issues of low priority and high ability to change. Although these are not as important, they may be worth pursuing since you have an ability to change them. The low priority issues with low ability to change probably don't deserve much attention.

APPLICATION QUESTIONS

1. Does your management understand and respect the role of a project manager? What could you do to help management understand it better?

2. What are the most important skills needed by a project manager? What can you do to better develop those skills?

3. Do responsibility, authority, and accountability function well in your organization? What can you do to keep them in balance?

4. Are the roles of team members in your current project well defined in writing? Do team members understand and work within those definitions? Could any current conflicts or confusion be cleared up by better role definition?

NOTE

1. J. Paul Getty, *How to Be a Successful Executive* (New York: Playboy Publishing, 1971).

DEFINING THE ROLES OF CLIENTS, CUSTOMERS, AND OTHER STAKEHOLDERS

This chapter discusses the roles of client, customer, and other stakeholders, and presents how to identify the individuals involved and how to define the roles they will play in the project.

For every project, it is important to clearly identify the client who requested the project, the stakeholders who have an interest in the project, and the customer who will use the product, service, process, or plan the project produces. For example, the president of a company may request a project to develop an order tracking system so that customers can look up the status of their orders on the Internet. The president is the client, the customers of the project are the people who will use the system to look up the status of their orders, and the stakeholders include others in the company who benefit from the system, such as the marketing or finance departments. Although you might think these roles are obvious, they often are not.

Some projects get into serious trouble because they have several clients (requesters) who each want something different from the project. Other projects have no clients who want to take responsibility for the project. Still other projects are in trouble because the customer is not well defined—believe it or not, sometimes no one knows who will use the product or service the project will create! Other projects fail because the needs of a stakeholder were not addressed.

CLIENT

The client is the person (or group) who requests the project. The client might come from a variety of sources—usually from within the organization, such as senior management, middle management, functional managers, or other project managers. Someone in the organization might generate an idea for a project, which then percolates to someone in upper management, who approves the project. In this case, who is the client? The individual who came up with the idea or senior manager who approved the project? The key is in determining who takes responsibility for the project and has the authority to give direction to the project by approving the project objectives and deciding on issues that arise.

It is critical that you identify the individual or group of individuals with the authority to approve the project objectives and give direction to the project. If senior management identifies a person to be the client for a project, be sure that management also delegates to that individual the authority to approve project objectives and make decisions for the project. Some project managers assume that an individual has such authority, only to find out much too late in the project that someone else actually has approval authority and has reversed earlier decisions!

Once you have identified the client, it is important to get a commitment of support for the project. Discussions with the client can confirm understanding of the project scope and its relative priority with other projects in the organization.

For each project, determine the following about the project's clients:

- Who (by name) is authorized to make decisions for the project?
- What access does the project manager have to this client?
- What approvals does the client require at which stages of the project?
- How will these approvals be obtained and how long will they take?
- Who (by name) has the authority to formally accept the project when it is completed?

If the project is cosponsored by more than one individual or group, it is important to define the role each will play in the decision-making process.

CUSTOMERS

The customer is the person or group of people who will use what the project is intended to provide—the product, service, process, or plan.

For each project, it is important to determine the following about the project's customers:

- Who are the customers who will use the outcome of the project?
- What access does the project team have to the customer?
- What approvals does the customer require at what stages of the project?
- How will these approvals be obtained and how long will they take?

Once you have identified your customers, it is important to get their commitment to support the project. If there is more than one group of customers, it is important to define the role each will play in the project.

It is important to identify and consult with the customer throughout the life of the project. Many projects fail because they do not meet the needs of the customer. You cannot assume that the needs of the customer have been fairly represented by the client when the project was approved. You must confirm and reconfirm customer needs as the project progresses to ensure that the final result meets the requirements.

OTHER STAKEHOLDERS

Most projects have stakeholders in addition to the client and customers, who have an interest in (and perhaps control over) the project. It is important to identify people who have a stake (interest) in the project and define their needs relative to the project. Stakeholders may be people in other departments, suppliers, contractors, vendors, government agencies, management, or stockholders in the company. Some projects fail because the needs of a stakeholder were not addressed. It is as important to manage the expectations of stakeholders as it is to manage the expectations of clients and customers. If a stakeholder has concerns about the project, he or she may be able to exert considerable influence on those who make project decisions.

For each project, it is important to determine the following about the project's stakeholders:

■ Who are the stakeholders in the project and what role will each play?

■ What access does the project team have to the stakeholders?

■ What approvals, review, or information does each stakeholder require at what stages of the project?

■ How will the approvals and reviews take place? How will the appropriate information be communicated?

If there is more than one group of stakeholders, it is important to define the role each will play in the project and get a commitment from each to support the project.

DEFINITIONS

Client. The person or group that requests a project, takes responsibility for the project, and has the authority to give direction to the project.

Customers. A person or group that will use what the project is intended to provide: the product, service, process, or plan.

Stakeholders. People who are involved in or impacted by the project, including clients, senior management, middle management, functional managers, project managers, project team members, customers, and vendors.

APPLICATION QUESTIONS

1. In your current project, can you clearly identify the client, customer(s), and other stakeholders?

2. Is your relationship with each of these people or groups clear and functional?

3. What can you do to better define these relationships?

CHAPTER 5

SETTING UP A PLANNING
AND CONTROL
SYSTEM

Planning and control go hand in hand. With a solid plan, a project manager can exercise proper control. Without a plan, there is nothing to compare progress against and project control is impossible. You cannot control without a plan.

Many organizations have no formal planning and control system. They operate using rationalizations:

"We have a set delivery date, so the project has to be completed by then."

"Budget as much as you think will be approved, then don't spend any more than that."

"Since the project must fit into our current environment, estimate its size to be no larger than we can handle."

This chapter discusses why a planning and control system is important and gives the basic components of such a system.

THE NEED FOR A PLANNING AND CONTROL SYSTEM

Some people put a minimum of effort into planning. They argue that since things invariably change during the life of the project, it is a waste of effort to make extensive up-front plans. The average organization spends only 5 percent of the total project effort on planning. More successful organizations spend up to 45 percent. A good rule of thumb is to spend at least 25 percent of the project effort in concept and development and 75 percent in implementation and termination.

Although it is true that factors might be introduced during the life of the project that necessitate minor or major adjustments to the plan, it is still important to have a solid plan in place. Without a solid plan, a project becomes even more chaotic in the face of change. If plans are made using project management software, it is easy to make adjustments to the plan as needed.

In an ideal world, a project would be planned and approved, then work would start and be completed according to the plan. In actual practice, however, you might have to adjust the plan throughout the life of the project. Therefore, any good planning and control system must be flexible enough to operate in the real world, but still be rigorous enough to provide control.

Some projects are managed in pieces. Because of time constraints or other factors, the project manager might have to develop a plan for only part of the project, get it approved, and begin that portion while other parts of the project are still in the planning stage.

Often, planning continues to some extent throughout the life of the project. Recognizing this reality, the successful project manager establishes a project management system that allows for adjustments to the plan as needed throughout the project's life.

ELEMENTS OF A PLANNING AND CONTROL SYSTEM

Figure 5-1 shows a generic model for a project planning and control system that allows a project to react to the changing conditions of the world.

- *Define the problem or opportunity.* The first phase of project planning is to clearly define the problem to be solved by the project or the opportunity of which the project will take advantage. This includes understanding the business reasons for the project and the client's motive in requesting it. This step is important because you will use it to keep the project focused and it might help you avoid damaging oversights that are not obvious to the client. As the project manager seeks to clarify the justification for the project, it may bring to light issues that the client was not able to see. (See Chapter 6 for information on defining the project.)

- *Establish project objectives.* Once you have clearly identified the problem or opportunity, the next step is to define the basic objectives of the project in terms of time, cost, and scope. These define the strategy (the overall approach to the project). They describe what the project will accomplish and ensure that customer requirements are met. (See Chapter 6 for more detailed information on establishing project objectives.)

Figure 5-1. Project planning and control system.

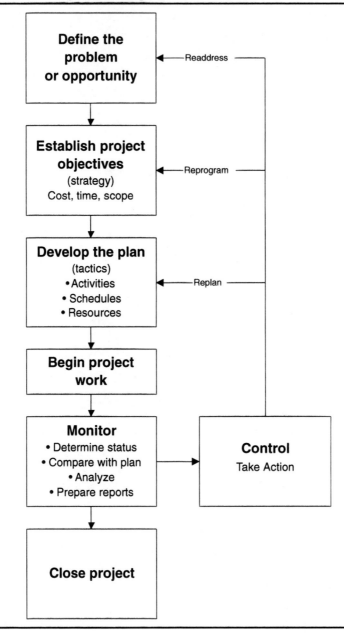

- *Develop the plan.* Within the framework of the project objectives, detailed plans are developed, including the activities, schedules, cost plans, and resources required to complete the project work. These are the tactics (the specific steps you take to implement the strategy). See Chapters 7–14 for information on developing project plans.

- *Begin project work.* When all plans are in place, approved, and communicated to project personnel, project work can begin. (See Chapter 16 for detailed information on initiating the project.)

- *Monitor.* As project work progresses, the project manager gathers status information and compares it to the plan to determine variances. These deviations from the plan are then analyzed to determine if corrective action should be taken. (Chapters 17 and 18 contain information on how to monitor and report on time, cost, and project scope.)

- *Control.* When necessary, the project manager takes corrective action to get the project back on track. Some deviations might require replanning the tactics by resequencing activities, rescheduling, rebudgeting, or reallocating resources. Larger deviations can necessitate reprogramming the strategy by renegotiating the basic project objectives of cost, time, and scope. In some cases, the situation might be serious enough to warrant readdressing the problem or opportunity to determine if it has been identified correctly and if the organization has the resources, expertise, and commitment necessary to handle it. Chapters 19 through 21 explain various aspects of project control.

- *Close project.* Chapter 22 explains the steps involved in formally closing a project.

Planning, monitoring, and controlling are not one-time events. They continue throughout the life of the project to refine and adjust to current conditions.

The remaining chapters take you through project planning and control step by step. Even though you might spend less effort on each step for a small project, it is important to address the concepts in each step.

To help you understand these steps, they are presented in a specific sequence. In reality, you might perform these steps several times throughout the project. For example, you might need to repeat some project planning steps in various phases of project execution. Steps can also overlap and interact in various ways. Every project will be different by definition. Therefore, you might need to apply some of the concepts in this book differently with each project.

APPLICATION QUESTIONS

1. How does the level of detail in the project plan affect your ability to control the project effectively? Do you currently plan to a sufficient level of detail?

2. Does your level of control match your plan? Are you currently managing at a greater level of detail than necessary?

3. Are you able to respond adequately to changes during the life of your project? What concepts from the planning and control model presented in this chapter could you implement in your current work?

CASE STUDY ❖❖❖❖❖❖❖❖❖

CXI Cellular

CXI Cellular of Salt Lake City, Utah, is an innovative manufacturer of cellular phone products. One of their bright, young engineers has designed a new cellular phone that is 25 percent smaller and lighter than any competitor's phone. The vice president of marketing has named Robert, his top salesman, to manage a project to engineer and manufacture the new product. He asks Robert to develop a schedule and budget and present it to the executive management team the following week.

When Robert present his plans to the executive management team, there is considerable discussion about whether the company should begin manufacturing the new phone. After the meeting, the chief operations officer (COO) of the company approaches Robert and asks him to move forward with the project and report directly to him. The COO asks to personally approve each project expense. In the meantime, the COO will work on getting the approval of the executive team.

Assignment: Based on the concepts presented in Chapters 1 through 5, what steps should Robert take to ensure the success of the project? Consider the following in your answer:

- Have project management principles been followed?
- Have roles and responsibilities been properly defined?
- Is Robert qualified?
- Has there been proper management approval?

(Suggested answers are given in Appendix A at the back of the book.)

SECTION 2

PLANNING THE PROJECT

SECTION OBJECTIVES

- Learn the steps in project planning to develop a defensible plan and logical schedule.

- Learn the tools needed to plan, schedule, and budget a project.

CHAPTER 6

DEFINING THE PROJECT

A clear project definition and detailed objectives are critical to the success of the project. If the definition and objectives are ambiguous, unrealistic, not agreed upon, or not written down, the project is in serious trouble before it begins. Whatever time and energy you need to define the project properly in the planning stage is much less than what it will cost to fix problems after the project is completed.

This chapter covers the first steps in project planning. It explains how to define the problem or opportunity that the project will address. It then discusses how to define the project objectives in terms of time, cost, and project scope. Finally, it recommends various reviews to ensure the integrity of the project plan.

DEFINING THE PROBLEM OR OPPORTUNITY

Although clients might spend hours discussing a proposed project, they might not think to communicate this insight to the project manager. The more the project manager understands the issues surrounding the project, the better chance the project has of success. For example, if a project involves the construction of a new plant, the project manager needs::

To know how the new plant will operate.

To understand the needs of the users of the new plant.

To understand why the client wants the new plant.

A clear view of what is involved in constructing the plant and what is expected of him.

To be sure the new plant will actually solve the problem at hand or appropriately address the presenting opportunity. If the problem or opportunity has not been correctly identified, the plant, even if constructed successfully, could be a failure!

The following actions help you define the problem or opportunity:

■ *Get from the client a clear definition of the problem to be solved by the project or the opportunity the project will take advantage of.* Work with the client to define it clearly and succinctly. This is important because it will be used to keep the project focused and may help you avoid damaging oversights that may not be obvious to the client.

■ *Determine the client's needs and wants.* It might take some time to help the client distinguish between needs and wants, but it is important to understand them because during the planning and budgeting process, some wants might have to be sacrificed in favor of needs when time and money are limited. If the client does not know what she needs or wants, document what you think she wants and ask her for a response. If the client can't commit, try a phased approach in which you agree to a smaller project that addresses the portion of the problem or opportunity she can agree on. Continue trying to define the larger project that can be undertaken when the preliminary project is completed.

- *Gather sufficient background information about the current situation.* Don't blindly accept information presented to you without appropriate confirmation. Well-intentioned stakeholders may mislead you because they only see things from their point of view. Be sure you investigate sufficiently to discover all the issues.

- *Learn and thoroughly understand the business reasons for the project and the client's motive in undertaking it.* This is important because it gives a basis for balancing the budget, schedule, and project scope. It might also help you capitalize on opportunities to improve the outcome of the project.

Types of Projects

It might help to categorize your project into one of these three types:

1. *Market-driven*: Producing a new product in response to market needs. A software company sells product and maintains market-share by creating quality programs that meet consumer needs.

2. *Crisis-driven*: A fast solution to a specific problem. In response to complaints about defective automobile tires, a manufacturer may quickly organize a project to manage the recall and replacement, as well as a public relations campaign.

3. *Change-driven*: the need to change operations to match the current environment or to be more effective. A retail sales company may approve a project to create an Internet commerce site to maintain its share of the market.

Understanding the purpose of the project is essential to comprehending the underlying needs so you can make appropriate tradeoffs in time, cost, and scope as you manage the project.

ESTABLISHING PROJECT OBJECTIVES

Once you have clearly identified the problem or opportunity, the next step is to define the basic objectives of the project, including *what is to be done* (specific end results), *how* (quantity, quality, or special requirements), *when* (deadline), and *how much* it will cost.

Clearly define the project objectives in terms of the desired end results. The project objectives should describe what the project will accomplish. Ask yourself, "If we achieve these stated objectives, will we consider the project a success?"

Consider the three main aspects of project objectives:

1. *Cost:* The money and resources required to get the job done, including people, equipment, and other allocations.

2. *Time:* the time required to get the job done.

3. *Scope:* A description of the features and functions of the end products or services to be provided by the project. Define all the deliverables and their features and functions. A *deliverable* is something provided at the end of the project, such as a product, service, process, or plan.

The project objectives must define the completion condition, describing what will and will not have been completed when the project is finished. This provides measurable criteria for project success.

These objectives define not only the project, but also the responsibilities of the project manager, who is measured against the objectives and held accountable for them. The project objectives must be SMART (*S*pecific, *M*easurable, *A*greed upon, *R*ealistic, and *T*ime-limited):

■   *Specific.* The objectives must be so clear and well defined that anyone with a basic knowledge of the project area can understand them. They must precisely define what the project will and will not do.

- *Measurable*. Objectives must be defined in measurable terms. If they cannot be measured, they are too ambiguous and fuzzy and you need to define them more clearly. To be successful, you must be able to measure and report on the progress.

- *Agreed upon*. The project manager, clients, and customers must agree on the project objectives. There must be agreement that the end result will solve the problem or respond to the opportunity defined.

- *Realistic*. The project objectives must be possible to achieve, given the available resources, knowledge, skills, and time. It might take some time and energy to negotiate project objectives that are realistic.

- *Time (cost) limited*. The objectives need to be framed within clear time (cost) goals. Define how much time (budget) is available and if there is any flexibility.

If the objectives are not SMART, keep working with them until they are. Objectives that are excessive can be detrimental to the project and the company. If project managers include too large a contingency (in an effort to insure their success), they run the risk of the project being too expensive and not being approved. Even if approved, such a project ties up large amounts of allocated funds that the company could better use elsewhere. The other extreme is an objective that is too lean. Project managers should include reasonable contingency in the objectives to give the project manager and team a fair chance for success. The project manager's task is to find a competitive, yet fair middle ground between these two extremes

Keep the Objectives in Balance

The triangle in Figure 6-1 shows the three principal aspects of a project: time, cost, and scope. The project manager's job is to keep these three aspects in balance.

Figure 6-1. The project objectives triangle.

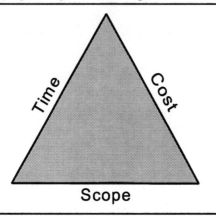

- If time is short, the resources (cost) must increase or scope must decrease, or both.

- If funds are short, the time can be extended or scope must decrease, or both.

- If the scope is large, the cost will be greater or the time must be extended, or both.

The frustration of trying to keep these three aspects in balance has led to the saying, "You can have it quick, cheap, or done right. Pick any two."

In an ideal world, project objectives would remain constant throughout the life of the project. In reality, however, the relative importance of each objective can change over time. It can be fatal to overemphasize the schedule when funds have become critical. The skillful project manager aims for a balanced emphasis, remaining flexible to adapt to new circumstances as they occur.

Consider the following issues as you balance cost, time, and scope.

Cost Considerations

Costs include the money and resources required to complete the project, including people, equipment, and materials. The client usually wants the project at the lowest cost possible. The budget for the project is approved based on the scope and schedule. The cost of the project is influenced by:

■ Specifications of the end products (such as levels of performance, quality, and reliability).

■ Compliance with governmental, institutional, or internal standards.

■ Technical requirements (such as a need to upgrade computer hardware) and administrative needs (such as a company's financial policies).

The project manager must establish performance standards to determine how to measure cost performance.

Time Considerations

The project schedule is easy to measure and is often given more attention than cost and scope.

■ The client usually wants the project NOW.

■ Clients might choose speed over cost and quality.

■ Project managers must balance the schedule with the project scope, budget, and resources available. Project managers must establish performance standards to determine how schedule performance will be measured.

Scope Considerations

Scope is often the most difficult project feature to define and on which to get agreement. The project scope is balanced with the time, budget, and resources available. It can increase over time ("scope creep") because of an inadequately defined problem or opportunity, overlooked details, unforeseen problems, or changes in the market or company.

A good scope statement clearly defines the end products or services. It describes what will and will not be completed at the end of the project. A complete scope statement includes technical specifications, performance requirements, facilities requirements, ground rules, constraints, exclusions, procedures, logistics, safety regulations, security issues, and environmental considerations. The scope statement should also consider how this project will change the way the company does business. What other aspects of the business will be affected by this project (in positive or negative ways)? What other departments will be involved with this project and what are the impacts on their resources?

The scope statement identifies which quality standards are relevant to the project and establishes performance standards to determine how to measure quality and compliance with scope specifications. Good quality is often difficult to produce because of the following factors:

- *Time and cost are key.* However, when too much emphasis is placed on time or cost and workers are up against tight time and cost restrictions, the quality of the final product often suffers. Modern approaches to quality control, such as Total Quality Management and Continuous Improvement, can help you balance quality with time and cost. When you measure only time and cost, you send the message that quality is less important. You should hold workers accountable for quality as much as for meeting the schedule and budget.

- *Work is becoming more complex and workers are becoming more expert.* The more technical the work, the more control the worker has over quality. Although all workers should accept responsibility for the quality of their work, those with highly specialized skills have an even greater responsibility for controlling quality when it is more difficult to find similar experts to review their work.

■ *Managers often lack the technical expertise to adequately supervise the work.*

■ *Quality is not planned.* If quality standards are not part of the initial plan, no amount of inspection will produce good quality.

Poor project quality leads to customer and management dissatisfaction, high maintenance costs, and increased outsourcing of critical functions.

Final Statement of Project Objectives

Once project objectives are defined, they should be clearly spelled out in a comprehensive *scope statement* that provides a documented basis for making future project decisions. It should include justification for the project, description of the product or service the project is to create, and a list of the project deliverables. This narrative description is shared with all stakeholders and project team members. As the project progresses, you might need to refine or revise the scope statement to reflect approved changes in scope.

PERFORMING PROJECT REVIEWS

Before a project is approved, a number of reviews are in order to be sure the project makes sense, that it is feasible, worthwhile, and not overly risky. The project manager can perform many of these reviews with input from management and the project team. In some cases, an independent appraisal can be helpful to reinforce the project manager's recommendations to management.

Conceptual Review

A conceptual review addresses these questions:

- Does the project fit within the mission, goals, and objectives of the company?
- Does this project support a specific business plan already in place?
- Will the project solve the stated problem or appropriately take advantage of the current opportunity?

This type of review is typically undertaken by a management team within the organization. It simply involves asking the hard questions of how the project fits within the organization's goals. However, if management is enamored with a project that has no place within the organization's objectives, it might take an objective third party to help them see the project's unsuitability.

Feasibility Study

A feasibility study addresses questions such as the following:

- How realistic is it to expect that the project can meet the stated objectives?
- How realistic are the project scope, budget, and time requirements?
- Can the appropriate resources be made available when needed to complete the project?
- Are sufficient funds available to complete the project?
- Does the organization have the technical expertise to accomplish the project?

A feasibility study can be done in house or by an external group. It can be useful to benchmark other organizations that have tried similar projects and learn from their failures and successes. A complex or high profile project might warrant a feasibility review by an independent party to be sure that the organization has the expertise and experience to handle the project. If a small utility company planned to build its first nuclear power plant, an extensive feasibility study by an independent party would certainly be in order.

Benefit–Cost Analysis

A benefit-cost review analyzes the costs and expected benefits of the project:

- What benefit will the organization get from completing this project?
- What is the value of the promised advantages, considering the amount of money involved, the time needed to complete the project, and the resources required?
- What is the project's value compared to other projects that could be done instead ("opportunity cost")?

A benefit-cost ratio provides a measure of the expected profitability of a project by dividing expected revenues by expected costs. A ratio of 1.0 means that expected benefits and costs are equal and you have a "break-even" project. Ratios less than 1.0 mean that costs are expected to exceed benefits and the project is not financially attractive. Ratios greater than 1.0 indicate profitable projects. The higher the ratio, the better the project. A major overhaul of a company's telephone system, which is expected to save the company $1 Million, has estimated costs of $800,000. Thus the overhaul project has a benefit-cost ratio of 1.25.

Benchmarking data from other organizations may be helpful to confirm the expected costs and returns.

Profitability Measures

You can make several quantitative measures that indicate the expected profitability of a project. Some of the more common are:

Payback period is defined as the number of periods (usually years) until cumulative revenues exceed cumulative costs; that is, the project has turned a profit. The shorter the payback period, the better. However, payback period does not identify the expected magnitude of the total profit.

Internal rate of return represents an average rate of return for the project, expressed as a percentage. A rate of 35 percent means you expect the project to return an average of 35 percent per year.

Return on assets is a measure of net profit divided by total assets.

Return on investment is a measure of net profit divided by total investment.

Return on sales is a measure of net profit divided by total sales.

Alternative Course of Action Review

A review of alternative courses of action is to ensure that the intended course of action is the best. It addresses these questions:

■ What other things could be done to solve the problem or take advantage of the opportunity instead of the approach taken by the proposed project?

■ What are the positive and negative consequences of each potential course of action?

■ What would happen if you take no action at all?

Opportunity Cost Review

Opportunity cost is the cost of choosing one among several alternatives (projects) and, therefore, giving up the potential benefits of another. If an organization chooses Project A (to manufacture a product that has an identified buyer and will generate a profit of $500,000) instead of Project B (to develop an experimental product with no identified buyer and a potential profit of $800,000), the organization is knowingly giving up the potential $800,000 for the more secure $500,000 profit. In selecting a project, the company commits finite resources, time, and energy. Therefore, it is important to take project selection seriously. Making poor choices in approving projects can cause the company to miss out on better opportunities.

Preliminary Risk Assessment

A risk assessment addresses these questions:

■ What could go wrong in the project and what are the potential consequences?

■ What are the uncertainties in the project?

■ What are the consequences if the project fails to meet its objectives?

■ What is the risk that it will not solve the problem?

The project manager and management need to determine whether the expected benefits of the project are worth the risk.

They might decide to modify certain aspects of the project to reduce risk.

Possible Review Outcomes

At the conclusion of the reviews, the client, project manager, and customer determine whether to:

- Proceed with the project.
- Change the project objectives.
- Drop the project.

You might need to repeat one or more of these reviews at certain points during the project to ensure the integrity of the project—especially if project objectives or assumptions change during the life of the project.

DEFINITIONS

Alternative course of action review. A review that identifies other ways to solve the problem or take advantage of the opportunity instead of the approach being taken by the proposed project.

Conceptual review. A review that determines whether the project fits within the organization's goals and whether the project will solve the stated problem or appropriately take advantage of the current opportunity.

Cost. The money and resources required to complete a project.

Deliverable. Something delivered at the end of a project, such as a product, service, process, or plan.

Feasibility study. A review that determines whether the project can realistically be accomplished.

Internal rate of return. A profitability measure that represents an average rate of return for the project, expressed as a percentage.

Objectives. The statement of cost, time, and scope required to complete a project.

Opportunity cost. The cost associated with choosing one project and, therefore, giving up the potential benefits of an alternative project.

Payback period. The number of periods (usually years) until cumulative revenues exceed cumulative costs; that is, the project has "turned a profit."

Preliminary risk review. An initial review of the potential risks involved in a project that determines whether the expected benefits of the project are worth the risk.

Return on assets. A measure of net profit divided by total assets.

Return on investment. A measure of net profit divided by total investment.

Return on sales. A measure of net profit divided by total sales.

Scope. A description of the features and functions of the end products or services to be provided by the project.

Scope creep. The tendency for scope to increase during the course of the project without proportionate increases in time or cost.

Scope statement. A narrative description of the project objectives, including justification for the project, a description of the product or service to be created, and a list of the project deliverables.

Time. The time required to complete a project.

APPLICATION EXERCISES

1. For your current project, draw a triangle and define the time, cost, and scope. Determine which of the three is currently the most important in your project. Re-read the considerations for time, cost, and scope and be sure you have considered all these issues in your project.

2. For your current project, perform a mini-conceptual review, feasibility study, benefit-cost analysis, alternative course of action review, opportunity cost review, and risk review. Write down the outcomes of each review showing the advantage (or disadvantage) of proceeding with this project.

APPLICATION QUESTIONS

1. Think of a past project that did not have a clear definition of the problem to be solved or the opportunity of which it was meant to take advantage. What are the dangers of proceeding with such a project?

2. What are the potential dangers of proceeding with a project that has no clear distinction between the client's *needs* and *wants*?

3. Give an example of a market-driven, crisis-driven, and change-driven project. How would your approach to each one differ in timing and priority?

4. Consider a past project that did not have project reviews. In retrospect, would you have made any changes in the project plan based on the outcome of such reviews?

CREATING A WORK BREAKDOWN STRUCTURE

After defining the objectives of the project, the next step is to break the project down into manageable pieces in a *work breakdown structure.*

A *work breakdown structure* defines the work to be completed in the project. It is a graphical representation (diagram) of the project showing its component parts. It provides definition to the project scope by showing the hierarchical breakdown of activities and end products that must be completed to finish the project.

The work breakdown structure is the basis for time estimating, resource allocation, and cost estimating and collection. If the work breakdown structure is faulty, all further planning will also be faulty. The work breakdown structure example in Figure 7-1 illustrates the Noah's Ark project.

Figure 7-1. Noah's Ark: work breakdown structure.

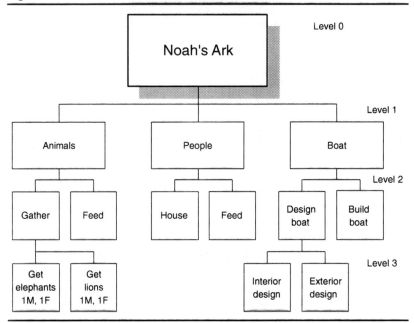

In preparing a work breakdown structure, keep the following in mind:

- *Use any category that makes sense for your project.* This might include components of the product, functions, organizational units, geographical areas, cost accounts, time phases, or activities.

- *Don't be constrained by sequence.* The diagram does not need to represent a logical or time sequence of events.

- *The diagram does not have to be symmetrical.* The number of levels might vary from one branch to the next. Break each branch down to the number of levels necessary to adequately define the project.

■ *Each box is a summary of the boxes in the levels below it.*

■ *The final box in each branch must end in a product or deliverable.* These must be measurable and definable in terms of an end result.

■ *The boxes in the lowest level are called work packages.* They represent the lowest level of detail you want to estimate, schedule, monitor, and control. They should represent eight to eighty hours of work. Each work package can be divided into specific activities. For each work package, describe the completion condition. Ask yourself what must be delivered to consider the activity finished.

■ *The sum total of boxes must represent the complete project.* You can leave nothing out. When all these deliverables are completed, will the project be done?

■ *The entire project team should be involved in developing the work breakdown structure.*

■ *When completed, you should review the work breakdown with the client and customers.* This is to ensure that it is complete and that it addresses their specific concerns.

When you develop a work breakdown structure, be sure to include these often overlooked activities:

■ *Project management.* Include the budgets and resources needed to manage the project. Include costs for the project manager, support staff, project office, and computer support.

■ *Documentation.* The documentation includes lessons learned, how the end product differs from the project plan (describe the "as built" condition), and how the end product functions.

■ *Product implementation.* Projects that deliver a great product or system can fail if they do not implement the product or system. This can include product delivery, user training, communication plans, or marketing plans.

- *End product evaluation.* Does the product perform as expected? Is the problem solved? Have you successfully taken advantage of the opportunity?

- *Project closure.* This includes the time, budget, and resources needed to close the project office, reassign project personnel, and close financial accounts (see Chapter 22).

- *Product retirement.* Include the plans to retire the product after its useful life. Organizations often require that the project that created the product or system include the plans—and even the budget and resources—to retire it at the end of its useful life.

DEFINITIONS

Work breakdown structure. A hierarchical diagram of activities and end products that organizes and defines all work to be completed in a project.

Work packages. The deliverables in the lowest level of the work breakdown structure. A work package can be divided into the specific activities to be performed.

APPLICATION EXERCISE

Create a work breakdown structure for your current project. Try to define it in no more than five levels.

APPLICATION QUESTION

Why should the entire project team be involved in creating the work breakdown structure? What are the dangers of one person creating a work breakdown structure?

❖ ❖ ❖
CHAPTER 8

ESTIMATING ACTIVITIES

The work packages (the boxes in the lowest level of the work breakdown structure) identify the specific activities that must be performed to complete the project. This chapter explains how to estimate the time and cost needed to complete each of these activities.

To properly estimate each activity, use the following three steps:

1. Referring to the work breakdown structure, ask the team members to complete an estimate sheet such as the one shown in Figure 8-1 for each work package. For each activity, develop a *statement of work* that succinctly defines the work to be accomplished in the activity. Each statement of work should be supported by the following:

■ Technical specifications of the end products, such as performance, quality, reliability, survivability, operability, and maintainability.

Figure 8-1. Activity estimate sheet.

Activity #_____ Title _____

Team Responsible _____

Team Leader _____

Statement of work: _____
_____
_____

Describe completion condition: _____
_____
_____

Describe assumptions, exclusions, constraints: _____
_____
_____
_____

Time Number of working days needed _____

Personnel
____ person hours of _____ skill group
____ person hours of _____ skill group
____ person hours of _____ skill group
____ person hours of _____ skill group
____ person hours of _____ skill group

Direct costs
item _____ cost $ _____ needed at day ___. ___ days to pay
item _____ cost $ _____ needed at day ___. ___ days to pay
item _____ cost $ _____ needed at day ___. ___ days to pay
item _____ cost $ _____ needed at day ___. ___ days to pay
item _____ cost $ _____ needed at day ___. ___ days to pay

Predecessor steps
This activity cannot begin until   Define if less than 100%
____ % of activity #____ is complete.   _____
____ % of activity #____ is complete.   _____
____ % of activity #____ is complete.   _____

Successor steps
This activity cannot begin until   Define if less than 100%
____ % of activity #____ is complete.   _____
____ % of activity #____ is complete.   _____
____ % of activity #____ is complete.   _____

Signature _____ Date _____

- Compliance with standards (governmental, institutional, international, and organizational).

- Project assumptions, constraints, and exclusions (a description of what is *not* included in this work package).

2. Ask the functional groups to document how the estimate is made, including assumptions and factors that might affect the validity of the estimate. For example, did the cost projections make allowances for the suppliers' annual price increases?

3. Review the estimate sheets and clear up discrepancies. For example, the estimate sheet requests both predecessor activities and successor activities. *Predecessor activities* are those that occur before the current activity and *successor activities* are those that occur after it. If the successor activity listed on one sheet does not show up as a predecessor activity on the other, check with the team members to make sure they have a common understanding of the intended workflow. (This is the reason for asking for both successor and predecessor activities on each sheet.) You might also want to compare relative material costs and person hours across various activities.

Although you might be tempted to skip over some information on this sheet, it is all essential. For example, the breakdown by skill group in the personnel section is necessary to identify the specific resources (personnel) needed (and to determine whether they are available when needed) and the cost for each (since people with different skill levels are typically paid different rates). The detail by item in the direct costs section can identify any costs overlap from one activity to the next. For example, if two activities each require purchasing the same equipment, the equipment cost can be charged to one activity for use by both. The identification of the number of days to pay for each cost is necessary to determine cash flow. Although it might appear redundant to ask each activity to list both the predecessor and successor activities, it can help isolate inconsistencies from one activity sheet to another. Not all activity workers view their interrelationships in the same way.

THE IMPORTANCE OF ESTIMATING

A novice project manager might believe it a waste of time to spend much effort estimating. However, experienced project managers recognize the importance of estimating as precisely as possible using the best estimating methods. For this reason, it is preferable to have estimates created by those who are experts in the field—preferably those who will actually work on the project.

Project estimating is difficult for two important reasons:

1. Estimating is not an exact science. Even under the best conditions, an estimate is only a prediction of the time, resources, and funds required to complete an activity.
2. By its very nature, a project is a unique undertaking and involves a degree of uncertainty.

Avoid creating estimates based on predetermined deadlines or budgets. Although those constraints might be real, you must be objective and honest in your assessment of the time, resources, and funds needed to complete your project. Once you complete the estimates, you can negotiate with the client to reconcile them with the project requirements. If they do not fit, it might be possible to adjust the project scope, deadline, or basic approach. It might also be possible to sequence the activities differently to complete the project in less time or to use alternative resources to complete the project at a lower cost.

ESTIMATING METHODS

The four most common estimating approaches are analogous, parametric, bottom-up, and simulation.

Analogous Approach

The analogous approach uses the actual costs and durations of previous, similar projects as the basis for estimating the current project. It uses historical information from the organization as well as industry standards. It is also called a *top-down* estimate, because it relies on information from the top row of activities of the work breakdown structure. It can be used to estimate projects with a limited amount of detailed information. For example, a project to implement a new accounts payable process in one company might be estimated by reference to a similar accounts payable process that was recently implemented in another company. Such an analogous approach is generally less costly than other approaches, but is also generally less accurate.

Parametric Modeling

Parametric modeling uses mathematical parameters to predict project costs. An example is residential home construction that is often estimated using a certain dollar amount per square foot of floor space. Complex examples can be found in the software development industry where one model uses thirteen separate adjustment factors, each of which has five to seven points. The cost and accuracy of parametric estimates vary widely.

Bottom–Up Estimate

This approach estimates the cost and duration of the individual work packages from the bottom row of activities of the work breakdown structure, then totals the amounts up each row until reaching an estimate for the total project. This approach can produce a more accurate estimate, but at a higher cost.

Simulation

In this approach, a computer calculates multiple costs or durations with different sets of assumptions. The most common is the Monte Carlo Analysis, in which a range of probable results is defined for each activity and used to calculate a range of probable results for the total project. Simulation can be more accurate than other types of estimates, and is principally used on large or complex projects.

PRECISION OF ESTIMATES

In early planning, you might be asked to provide a preliminary or conceptual estimate, also called an *order-of-magnitude estimate*. This level of estimate is usually −25 percent to +75 percent. Thus, the range of the order-of-magnitude for a $50,000 estimate would be $37,500 to $87,500. Later, at the project approval stage when more definition is available, you might be asked for a budget estimate, which usually ranges from −10 percent to +25 percent. During project planning, when well-defined specifications are available for individual activities, you might need to provide definitive estimates that can be used for bid proposals or contract negotiations. Definitive estimates usually use a bottom-up approach, and typically range from −5 percent to +10 percent.

The more specific the details, the better the estimate, and therefore the greater the chance of meeting the project objectives. However, the greater the detail, the greater the cost and time to get the estimate and the less time and budget will be left to accomplish the project.

To increase the accuracy and consistency of your estimates, you might want to:

■ Use several independent techniques and sources.

■ Compare and iterate estimates. For example, you might ask two independent groups to use the same estimating method, or one group to use two different methods. Investigate the differences among the estimates and adjust the estimating approach to what is appropriate for your project. An analysis after the project is important to determine if your approach was valid. This helps you learn from each project and produce a better estimate on the next.

Underestimating Activities

Managers often underestimate activities, and projects run over budget and over schedule. Here are some common reasons:

- Team members are usually optimistic and desire to please. They might say what they think the project manager wants to hear.

- People might underestimate the amount of nonproductive time in a day (such as personal distractions, fatigue, interruptions, meetings, administrative tasks, sick leave, vacations, training, crisis management, and so on).

- Workers might be overly optimistic about the number of calendar days it takes to complete the number of work hours estimated.

- People tend to have incomplete recall of previous experience. They remember successes better than failures and tend to forget pain.

- Team members might not be familiar with the complete scope of the project when they make their estimates.

- Workers might have no experience with this activity to draw upon.

Before beginning the estimating process, it may be helpful to discuss these issues with all who will be involved so they can deal with them appropriately. Peer reviews during the process may also help identify underestimating.

Inflating Estimates

Novice project managers might be tempted to inflate estimates so they can come in ahead of schedule and under budget. However, from the point of view of resource utilization, projects running ahead of schedule may be as bad as projects running behind schedule. If a new office building is completed six months ahead of schedule because of an inflated estimate, the building may sit vacant until tenants are able to occupy it. The owner may lose months of rental revenue that he otherwise could have received had he known when the building would be available and had scheduled the tenants for occupancy sooner. Inflating the estimates defeats the purpose of planning. Expert project managers have a few projects that come in ahead of schedule and under budget, a few behind schedule and over budget, and many that come in close to the plan.

Project managers should estimate what they think the project will actually cost, then add a reasonable contingency amount for unknown variables. The percentage of contingency varies depending on the kind of activity, environment, and degree of risk. There is no magical percentage to plan as a contingency. A 3 to 5 percent contingency might be sufficient for work that is fairly routine, whereas 10 to 15 percent might be appropriate for unusual work that has many unknowns. Managers can establish a contingency reserve within the project to be drawn upon to reduce the impact of missing cost or schedule objectives.

Estimating Familiar vs. New Work

If the work to be estimated is familiar, the work breakdown structure is also familiar and you can rely on performance standards, historical databases, established guidelines, and standard costs. You can improve performance on these projects over time. However, how do you reliably estimate new work or work that uses new technology? Consider the estimating issues shown in Figure 8-2.

Figure 8-2. Estimating familiar vs. new work.

	Familiar work	*New work*
Familiar technology	■ Needs accurate performance data. ■ Draw on performance history and measure performance improvement. ■ Easiest type of project work to plan.	■ Difficult to predict since activities may be different. ■ No performance history available or not useful. ■ High probability of estimates being understated. ■ Needs frequent project reviews and estimate revisions.
New technology	■ Performance history needs to be adjusted for the complexity of technology. ■ Important issue is the similarity of activities. ■ New activities required by the technology are difficult to estimate.	■ Use a group of experts to produce the estimate. ■ Very short planning horizons. ■ No performance history available or not useful. ■ Needs close monitoring and frequent replanning.

Weighted Estimating Formulas

If the activity is well-known and has little risk, a single estimate might be sufficient. However, if the activity is less well-known or the risk is higher, you might want to gather three estimates: a *most likely* estimate (given what you expect to happen), an *optimistic* estimate (if everything goes very well), and a *pessimistic* estimate (if things go poorly). You can then combine the three estimates to calculate the average expected duration or cost for the activity, using the following formula, based on principles of statistics:

$$\text{Estimated time} = \frac{optimistic + (4 \times most\ likely) + pessimistic}{6}$$

This formula calculates the PERT *(Program Evaluation and Review Technique)* *weighted average,* sometimes called *expected time.* This estimate accounts for the uncertainty and variability inherent in project work and provides a risk-adjusted estimate. It works equally well for both time and cost estimates.

Range Estimates

Traditionally, we consider budgets as fixed amounts. For example, we estimate $3,875,350 to complete the project, or we budget $459,750 for the annual operation of a functional department. However, in today's business world, it can be more helpful to view functional budgets as limitations ("We expect to spend $450,000 this year to operate the functional department, and will spend no more than $475,000."). In the same vein, we view budgets as targets within limitations ("We estimate the project to cost $3.8 to $4 million, not to exceed $4.2 million."). Using a target range for projects is especially useful for the following types of projects:

- Large projects
- Projects with greater risk
- Projects that are more difficult to define, such as research projects

Consider an aircraft flight plan. Because of factors beyond the pilot's control (air currents, temperature variations, side winds, etc.), the flight plan allows a range rather than a fixed course, as illustrated in Figure 8-3. The pilot's target is to stay in the center of the band, but as long as he stays within the eight-mile wide band, he is within the accepted tolerance limits. The difference between the target and the limit is the contingency. The pilot takes periodic readings to determine his position from the center of the band and makes course corrections during the trip to ensure that the plane's flight stays within the accepted limits. The pilot also analyzes the corrections he makes

Figure 8-3. Range limits for an aircraft flight plan.

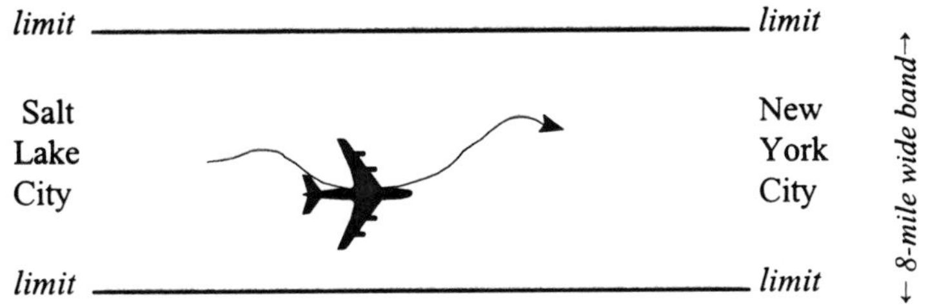

to determine if there are trends for which he needs to account. In today's business world, many accounting and budgeting procedures are changing from fixed-amount methods to ranges or limitations.

Activity-based costing uses accounting and budgeting methods that relate all work activity in the organization to projects. This forces the company to focus on its end products (sales and services) and gives managers a better picture of the real profitability of the company's products and services.

Rolling Wave Estimates

In some projects, detailed estimates might be valid for only three months. In an environment where the cost of materials changes rapidly, for example, you might want to calculate detailed estimates for only the coming three months. As you get closer to the conclusion of the project, the nondetailed ("gross") portion of the estimate grows progressively smaller and you can forecast the outcome of the project with increasing accuracy (see Figure 8-4).

Rolling wave estimates are especially useful for engineering, information technology, and research and development projects because subsequent phases of the project are dependent on requirements defined in earlier phases. For example, you may not be able to plan the second phase of an engineering project in

Figure 8–4. Rolling wave estimate.

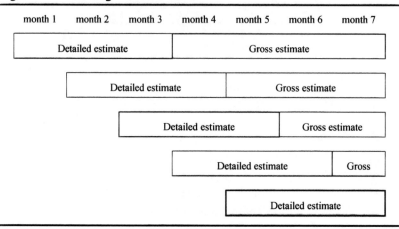

much detail until you gather the test results at the end of the first phase. Those test results provide the necessary requirements to plan the second phase in detail.

Rolling wave estimates present an increased risk. If the project is long, it might not be efficient to break later activities into great detail from the beginning. A five-year research project to find a drug for treating an illness is a good example of a project that is difficult to plan in detail from the beginning. Planning too much detail may be a waste of effort because you may end up reworking these activities because of information gathered later or because the project changes as it progresses.

TYPE OF CONTRACT

When estimates depend on the performance of outside vendors or contractors, the type of contract is critical. For example, a fixed-price contract provides greater confidence in the estimate than does a cost-plus contract. Different types of contracts might be appropriate in different circumstances. There are three basic types of contracts: fixed price, unit price, and cost plus.

Fixed-Price Contract

With a fixed-price (also called a *lump sum*) contract, the vendor agrees to do the total work for a fixed price. The vendor assumes the risk of unforeseen problems in exchange for a larger profit. This type of contract is appropriate when dealing with unknown vendors or when the project manager anticipates the work is risky.

Unit-Price Contract

With a unit-price contract, the vendor agrees to a preset amount per unit of service (such as $90 per hour for professional services or $1.80 per cubic yard of earth removed), and the total value of the contract is a function of the quantities needed to complete the work.

Cost-Plus Contract

With a cost-plus contract, the vendor agrees to do the work for the cost of time and materials, plus an agreed-upon amount of profit. Cost-plus contracts, also called *time-and-materials* contracts or *cost-reimbursable* contracts, are used when dealing with in-house providers or trusted vendors over whom you have great control. With these contracts, the project manager assumes the risk of unforeseen conditions, but is usually able to complete the project at a lower cost.

Incentives

Incentives or awards, such as completing work before a given date or controlling costs to a given level, can be included in any of the above contract types. If final project costs are less than the expected costs, for example, both the buyer (the organization) and the seller (the contractor) might benefit in the cost savings based on a pre-negotiated sharing formula. An 85/15 sharing formula means the buyer absorbs 85 percent of the risk and the seller absorbs 15 percent. If the expected project cost is $1,000,000 and the actual cost is only $800,000, the $200,000 savings is split 85/15: the seller gets $30,000 and the buyer saves $170,000. A cost-plus contract with an incentive, for example, is referred to as a *cost-plus-incentive* contract.

WORK ENVIRONMENT AND SKILL LEVEL

When preparing estimates, it is also important to consider the work environment and the skill level of those who will do the work.

- Adjust the estimates depending on situations in the work environment that make it more or less difficult to complete the work.

- Increase estimates if workers will be distracted by other responsibilities or interrupted by other projects. If you change the amount of time a worker spends on a project from 100 percent to 50 percent, it takes the worker more than twice as long to complete it because time is wasted shifting between projects.

- Increase the estimates when using less-skilled workers or workers with whom you have little experience.

USING PROJECT MANAGEMENT SOFTWARE

Hundreds of computer software products exist to help you manage project estimates and other plans more accurately and in much less time.

Most software pays for itself in one six-month project. Managers can use project management software to store and update project plans and also to enter status information once project work begins.

Using computer software is not a substitute for practical management and control of project schedules and costs. A common error is to automate a function that has been a problem in the past, mistakenly believing that computerization will solve the problem. Automating a problem only helps you make the same mistake faster and more efficiently. Management problems should be identified and solved before implementing computer software, the value of which is in the efficiency in updating and processing information.

Project management software cannot establish project objectives, define project tasks or dependencies, determine and manage project constraints, or estimate timelines and budgets. Software can provide data that is easy to modify and update, run "what-if" scenarios, make complex calculations and determine variances, present information in easy-to-read formats, and make it immediately available to many people.

Consider the following when you choose project management software:

Ease of use. How easy is it to learn and to use? Does the software have a good balance of powerful features and ease of use? Although the software might make it easy to begin projects quickly, will it still have the power you need when you are ready for it? Tutorials are helpful. Clear documentation and context-sensitive online help are a must.

Project planning. The best programs let you generate activity outlines and summaries, such as work breakdown structures, organization breakdown structures, and resource breakdown structures. They allow you to create custom calendars for both activities and resources. They also provide planning tools to do "what-if" analyses to evaluate alternative scheduling scenarios.

Resource management. If you manage several projects that use common resources, be sure the software can manage the projects by sharing a central resource pool. This macro view of resource availability helps maximize available resources by resolving scheduling conflicts and working within resource limitations.

Baseline comparison. As your project moves from the planning stage to the operational stage, you will likely need to adjust schedules and budgets from time to time. A good project management system maintains the original schedules and budgets as a baseline for future comparison.

Reporting. Does the system have the power to produce custom reports or are you limited to standard, pre-programmed reports? How easy is the report writer to use?

Multiple projects. Some software programs have a limit on the number of projects or activities in a given project. Be sure the software can handle your workload. Also determine how the software merges or groups projects for analysis. If you have dependencies across projects, look for software that maintains an independent file for each project, performs true critical path calculations across projects, and automatically incorporates schedule constraints in individual project files. This helps avoid scheduling errors and resource conflicts.

Customization. Look for software that lets you customize screen layouts, spreadsheets, and diagrams to your company preferences. Will you have to change your procedures to suit the program's limitations or is the program flexible enough to match your processes?

Access to project data. Can project data be shared with other software, such as spreadsheets, databases, and word processing programs?

Graphics. Can the program produce the graphs, charts, and diagrams you regularly use, or will you have to export the data to another software product to produce them?

Product support. Can you expect professional technical support from the vendor? Does the vendor understand project management? Can the vendor help you apply the product to your needs?

DEFINITIONS

Activity estimate sheet. A form used to gather information needed to estimate a project activity.

Analogy estimate. A method of estimating that uses the actual costs and durations of previous, similar projects as the basis for estimating the current project. Also called *top-down estimating.*

Bottom-up estimate. A method of estimating that sums the cost and duration of the individual work packages.

Contingency reserve. A planned amount used to allow for future situations that might be planned for only in part. Intended to reduce the impact of unknown variables on cost, schedule, or both.

Cost-plus contract. A contract in which the vendor agrees to do the work for the cost of time and materials, plus an agreed amount of profit. Also called *time-and-materials* contract and *cost-reimbursable* contract.

Fixed-price contract. A contract in which the vendor agrees to do the total work for a fixed price.

Parametric estimate. A method of estimating that uses mathematical parameters (such as a dollar amount per square foot) to predict project costs.

Predecessor activity. An activity that occurs before another activity in a project.

Rolling wave estimate. A method of estimating that provides a gross estimate for the entire project and periodically calculates detailed estimates for the next short period of time.

Simulation estimate. A method of estimating that calculates multiple costs or durations with different sets of assumptions.

Statement of work. A narrative description of the work to be accomplished in a project. A general statement of work might apply to the entire project, while a more specific statement of work might apply to a project activity or the work of an individual team member.

Successor activity. An activity that occurs after another activity in a project.

Unit-price contract. A contract in which the vendor agrees to a preset amount per unit of service (for example, $90 per hour).

APPLICATION EXERCISES

1. Complete an estimate sheet for one activity of your current project.

2. Determine which estimating approach is most appropriate for this activity and describe how you determined the estimate.

3. Prepare three time estimates for the activity: a most likely, an optimistic, and a pessimistic estimate. Then use the PERT weighted-average estimating formula to calculate a risk-adjusted estimate.

APPLICATION QUESTIONS

1. Why is estimating not an exact science?

2. How precise do the estimates need to be in your current project?

3. Why might different estimating approaches be appropriate under different conditions? How can you help your organization understand this?

4. Why do people tend to underestimate activities?

5. How would your approach to estimating new work be different from estimating familiar work?

6. Would it be more helpful in your organization to use a range rather than a fixed estimate? Why or why not?

7. What type of contract is appropriate for your project? Why?

8. Does your organization typically use one type of contract in all situations? Would it be more appropriate to use different types? Why?

❖❖❖
CHAPTER 9

SEQUENCING ACTIVITIES

An important part of project planning is determining the logical work flow of the various activities you identified in the work breakdown structure. This chapter explains how to create a *network diagram,* which is a graphical flow plan of the activities that must be accomplished to complete the project. The diagram illustrates which activities must be performed in sequence (after the previous activity is completed) and which can be done in parallel (at the same time). The diagram shows the planned sequence of steps, with all dependencies and relationships. It shows what is logically possible without the constraints of resource availability.

DIAGRAMMING METHODS

Bar charts (such as Gantt charts) are helpful ways of communicating project information, but because they don't show the logical relationships among activities, they are not as helpful in planning. (See Chapter 11 for a discussion of using Gantt charts after a project schedule has been established.) Project managers commonly use three network diagramming methods that show the logical relationships among activities: *precedence diagramming method, arrow diagramming method,* and *conditional diagramming method.*

Precedence Diagramming Method

Precedence Diagramming Method (PDM) is also referred to as *activity-on-node* because it shows the activities in a node (box) with arrows showing dependencies. (See Figure 9-1.) It is the most common form used in project management software packages and is the method illustrated in this book. This method makes it easy to describe in each box as much detail as you want about the activity.

Arrow Diagramming Method

A less common diagramming method is to represent the activities on arrows and connect them at nodes (circles) to show the dependencies. These are called *arrow diagrams* or *activity-on-arrow.* Figure 9-2 diagrams the same project as in Figure 9-1. With this method, it is more difficult to provide detailed infor-

Figure 9-1. Precedence diagramming method.

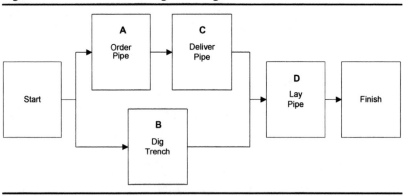

Figure 9-2. Arrow diagramming method.

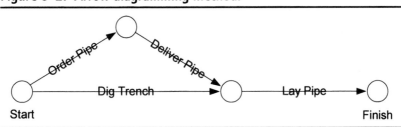

mation about each activity because text must be placed on the arrows or in footnotes at the bottom.

Conditional Diagramming Method

Project managers use this method in specialized situations, such as research and development projects, where some activities might be performed more than once, only partially, or not at all. This method would be helpful in an investigational drug study where you would not know up front the number of trial test periods needed to gather sufficient data to complete the study.

CREATING A NETWORK DIAGRAM

Application Exercise

Prepare a network diagram by using the following steps:

1. *For each work package activity in the work breakdown structure, determine the logical relationships (also called precedence relationships) with other activities.* That is, determine which activities depend on other activities. Some dependencies are mandatory, being inherent in the nature of the work. These often involve physical limitations, such as the framework of a house being dependent

on a foundation being completed first. Other dependencies are discretionary, and are defined by the project team. These are preferred dependencies based on "best practices." Remember that an activity may depend on more than one other activity. In Figures 9-1 and 9-2, for example, the task *lay pipe* is dependent on two tasks: *deliver pipe* and *dig trench*.

2. *Arrange the activities into logical sequences or paths.* Place activities that are not physically or logically dependent on each other in separate paths. Each activity in a given path must be dependent on the activity that immediately precedes it. In other words, an activity cannot begin until its preceding activities have been completed.

3. *Review each path to be sure it makes sense.* The activities in a given path build on each other. All paths come together at the end of the project. No activity can lead to a dead end. If you discover you have overlooked an activity that should be part of the project, go back and add it to the work breakdown structure.

UNDERSTANDING A NETWORK DIAGRAM

As shown in Figure 9-1, activities A and B start at the beginning of the project. Activity A must be completed before C can begin and activities C and B must both be completed before activity D can begin. This example has been simplified for the purpose of illustration. In reality, if part of the pipe is delivered and part of the trench is dug, that portion of pipe can be laid. However, this diagram shows that all pipe must be delivered and the entire trench dug before pipe laying can begin.

Activity Relationships

Network diagramming requires that you indicate the relationships between the activities. All activities are related in some direct way and may be further constrained by indirect relationships.

Direct Relationships

All activities in the network diagram must be linked using one of the relationships shown in Figure 9-3.

Indirect Relationships

Activities can be further defined using the constraints shown in Figure 9-4.

As an example, let's assume we are to construct a pump station. Figure 9-5 lists the project activities identified in the work breakdown structure. The duration of each activity was identified in the estimating process and the preceding activities were determined in the logical process of sequencing the activities. The network diagram in Figure 9-6 shows the planned sequence of steps and interdependencies.

DEFINITIONS

Finish-to-finish activity relationship. A dependency between activities where one activity must finish before the other can finish.

(text continues on page 104)

Figure 9-3. Direct relationships among project-related activities.

Finish to Start	Activity **A** must finish before activity **B** can begin.
Start to Start	Activity **A** must begin before activity **B** can begin.
Start to Finish	Activity **A** must begin before activity **B** can finish.
Finish to Finish	Activity **A** must finish before activity **B** can finish.

Figure 9-4. Indirect relationship constraints among project-related activities.

Must start on . . .	Activity must start on a given date.
Must start before . . .	Activity must start before a given date.
Must start after . . .	Activity must start after a given date.
Must finish on . . .	Activity must finish on a given date.
Must finish before . . .	Activity must finish before a given date.
Must finish after . . .	Activity must finish after a given date.

Figure 9-5. Activities to construct a pump station.

Activity no.	Activity description	Duration in days	Preceding activity
1	Start	0	
2	Mobilize	2	1
3	Survey	1	2
4	Grade site	2	2
5	Trench footings	5	3, 4
6	Form and pour concrete	5	5, 8
7	Cure concrete	8	6
8	Concrete and material design	5	1
9	Spec prefab metal building	4	1
10	Plumbing materials, pump	5	1
11	Electrical materials, lights, panel	5	1
12	Install pump	7	7, 9, 10
13	Erect structural steel	4	7, 9, 10
14	Install roofing and siding	5	13
15	Install lights and panels	3	11, 14
16	Test pump	2	12
17	Paint	3	15
18	End	0	16, 17

Figure 9–6. Network diagram for construction of a pump station.

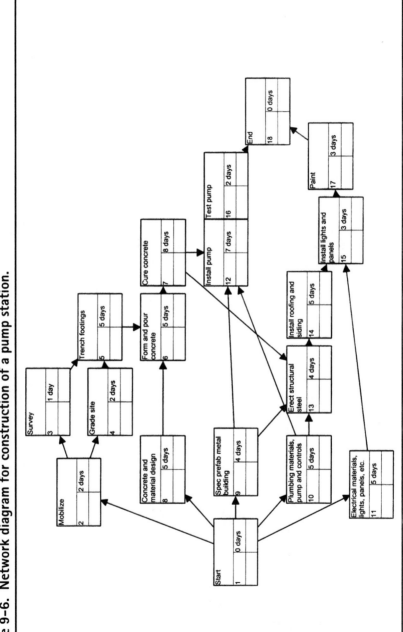

Finish-to-start activity relationship. A dependency between activities in which one activity must finish before the other can begin.

Network diagram. A graphical flow plan of the activities that must be accomplished to complete the project. It shows the planned sequence of steps, time requirements, interdependencies, and interrelationships. Also called *precedence diagram.*

Parallel activities. Two or more activities that occur at the same time. Also called *concurrent* or *simultaneous* activities.

Sequential activities. Two or more activities that occur one after the other. Also called *consecutive* activities.

Stakeholders. People who are involved in or impacted by the project.

Start-to-finish activity relationship. A dependency between activities where one activity must begin before the other can finish.

Start-to-start activity relationship. A dependency between activities where one activity must begin before the other can begin.

APPLICATION EXERCISES

1. A husband and wife have decided to have a picnic at the lake. For each of the activities listed in Figure 9-7, determine the preceding activity and draw a network diagram.

    (The answers are given in Appendix A at the back of the book.)

Figure 9-7. Picnic at the lake: planned activities.

Activity Description	Person Responsible	Duration (mins.)	Preceding activity
1. Decide on trip	Husband & wife	2	
2. Get money from bank	Husband	12	
3. Boil eggs	Wife	10	
4. Make egg sandwiches	Wife	10	
5. Load car	Husband & wife	5	
6. Drive to lake	Husband & wife	30	

2. Draw a network diagram for your current project. Identify the direct relationships between each activity.

APPLICATION QUESTIONS

1. Do you draw a network diagram for all your projects?
2. What can you do to help your organization understand the value of a network diagram?

CASE STUDY ❖❖❖❖❖❖❖❖❖

<u>Geebold Manufacturing</u>

Five months ago, the board of directors of Geebold Manufacturing approved the building of a new facility to manufacture a new line of clothing. The company has already selected the project manager and the project team.

Ann, the project manager, has spent the past five months planning the project. She carefully defined the project in terms of cost, time, and scope, and obtained the approval of the board of directors on the statement of work.

Working diligently, she created a work breakdown structure to the best of her knowledge. The diagram contains over one hundred boxes in eight levels. Some of the work packages represent two to three hours of work and a few represent 150 hours work. She then estimated each of the activities using an analogous approach, drawing on plans she discovered of a similar facility the company planned three years ago but never completed.

Ann then drew a graphical network diagram including each of the work packages from the work breakdown structure. The diagram showed the sequence of activities and their interrelationships. Ann is now ready to select the project team and get the project rolling.

What has Ann done correctly? If you were the project manager, what would you do differently?

(Suggested answers are given in Appendix A at the back of the book.)

10

CALCULATING THE CRITICAL PATH

Mathematical techniques for calculating schedules appeared in the early 1950s with the PERT (Program Evaluation and Review Technique) and CPM (Critical Path Method). These techniques allowed project managers to plan, analyze, and control complex projects. The United States Navy, Booz-Allen, and Lockheed developed PERT for the Polaris program. PERT emphasized meeting schedules with cost flexibility. It was developed to estimate project duration for projects with a high degree of uncertainty in the individual activity duration estimates. PERT provided three time estimates for each activity: a *most likely* (m), an *optimistic* (o), and a *pessimistic* (p), which were computed as follows with an emphasis on the most likely:

$$\text{Estimated time} = (o + 4m + p) / 6$$

Although the PERT weighted-average estimate formula is still used, the entire PERT system is seldom used today.

The most common method used today is the CPM, which was developed by DuPont and Remington Rand for planning and scheduling plant maintenance and construction programs. It emphasizes controlling cost and leaving the schedule flexible.

USING THE CRITICAL PATH METHOD

Using the network diagram (Chapter 9), the next step is to determine the critical path. The *critical path* is the path through the network that takes the longest total time. It therefore determines the earliest possible time the project can be completed.

It is important to know the activities that are on the critical path. These activities are not inherently more important than the others, but they have the least scheduling flexibility. Critical path tasks require more careful monitoring because if they are not completed on time, the project will be late—unless subsequent activities are completed in less than the scheduled time.

The critical path method calculates the following dates for each activity:

- *Early start* is the earliest date the activity can begin.
- *Late start* is the latest date the activity can begin and still allow the project to be completed on time.
- *Early finish* is the earliest date the activity can end.
- *Late finish* is the latest date the activity can end and still allow the project to be completed on time.

For activities on the critical path, the early and late start (and early and late finish) are the same.

Another important concept to understand is *float* (also known as *slack, float,* and *path float*). Float is the time an activity can slip without delaying the project. It is equal to the difference between the early start and late start (or the difference between the early finish and late finish). Activities on the critical path generally have zero float. Activities on the same noncritical path have the same, shared float. (*Free float* is the amount of time an activity can be delayed without delaying the early start of any immediately succeeding activities.)

One final concept is *lag,* which is the time delay between activities. A lag of 5 between activities A and B (with a finish-to-start relationship) means that B cannot start until five days after A is finished; for example, the curing time needed after pouring concrete. Lag can also be expressed as a negative number, in which case it indicates an overlap in the activities. In the same example, a lag of –5 means that B can begin five days before A is finished. Negative lag (overlap) is also called *lead.*

The network diagram in Figure 10-1 again shows the example of the pump station from Chapter 9. The critical path is identified by activities in heavy boxes.

CRITICAL PATH CALCULATIONS

Project management software (see Chapter 8) is commonly used for critical path calculations. Once the manager enters the activity durations and preceding activities, the program determines the critical path, early start, early finish, late start, late finish, and float. This saves significant time creating the original schedule and subsequent reschedules. Some programs also run *simulations* that calculate a range of possible schedule or cost outcomes by "performing" the project multiple times using different sets of assumptions. The most common is Monte Carlo Analysis, in which a distribution of probable results is defined for each activity and used to calculate a range of possible outcomes. Simulations are more accurate than PERT and CPM because they provide more predictive estimates as a result of the multiple project outcomes simulated.

Figure 10–1. Critical path for construction of a pump station.

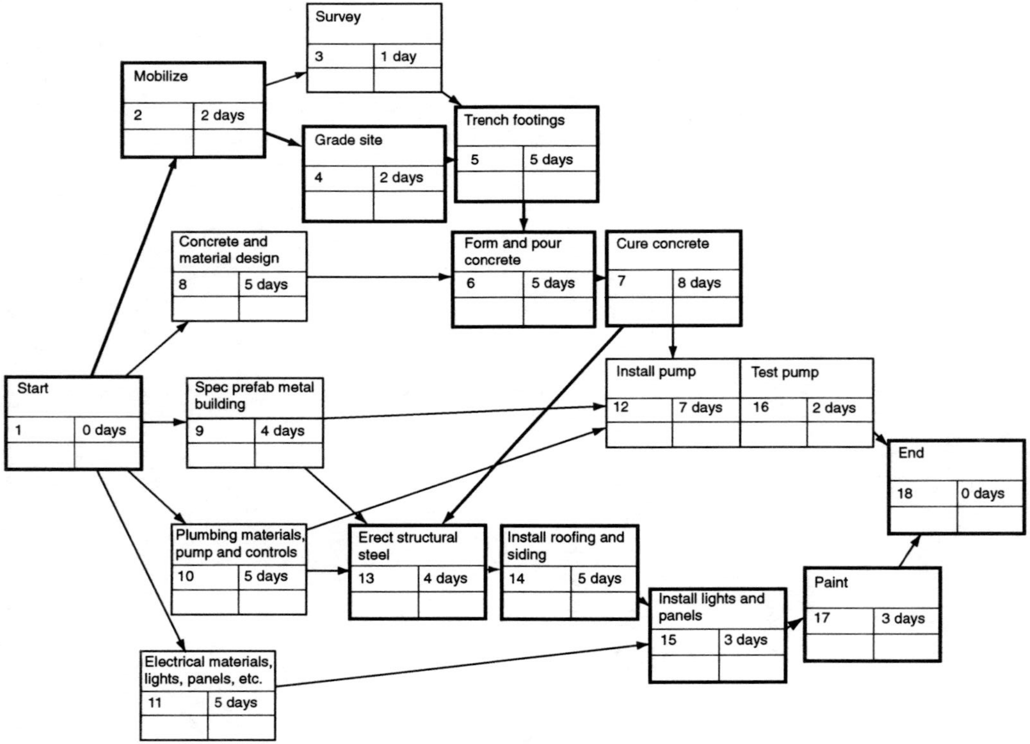

The following sections explain how to manually calculate the early start, early finish, late start, late finish, float, and critical path. We will use the example of the picnic at the lake from Chapter 9 (see Figure 10-2).

Calculating Early Start and Early Finish

A forward pass calculation is used to determine the early start and early finish times for activities. The calculations, which are expressed as units of time (such as hours, days, or weeks), do not represent scheduled dates. Calculate the early start and finish times as follows:

1. Write 0 for the early start time for the first activity.

2. Add the duration to the early start time to calculate the early finish time. Write these calculations in each box. The early finish time of one activity becomes the early start time for the next activity.

3. Repeat Step 2 for each activity working from the beginning of the network to the end.

Calculating Late Start and Late Finish

A backward pass through the network computes the late start and late finish times for activities as follows:

1. For late finish of the last activity, write the latest time you want the project to finish (generally, this would be the early finish time for the last activity computed from the forward pass).

Figure 10-2. Picnic at the lake: planned and preceding activities.

Activity Description	Person Responsible	Duration (mins.)	Preceding activity
1. Decide on trip	husband & wife	2	none
2. Get money from bank	husband	12	1
3. Boil eggs	wife	10	1
4. Make egg sandwiches	wife	10	3
5. Load car	husband & wife	5	2, 4
6. Drive to lake	husband & wife	30	5

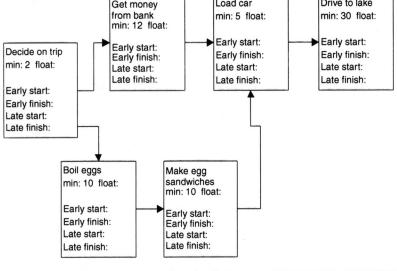

2. Subtract the duration from the late finish to calculate the late start time. Write these calculations in each box. The late start time of one activity becomes the late finish time for the previous activity.

3. Repeat Step 2 for each activity working from the end of the network to the beginning.

Calculating Float

Float (slack) is calculated for each activity by subtracting the early finish from the late finish. Float is the amount of time the activity can slip without delaying the project finish date.

Calculating Critical Path

The critical path can be determined by finding the path of activities that have zero float. Figure 10-3 shows the calculations for the picnic at the lake. The critical path is shown with heavy boxes.

DEFINITIONS

Critical activity. An activity on the critical path.

Critical path. The path through the network that takes the longest total time, and therefore determines the earliest possible time the project can be completed. All activities on this path have zero float; the early and late start (and early and late finish) are the same.

Early finish. The earliest date an activity can end.

Early start. The earliest date an activity can begin.

Float. The time an activity can slip without delaying the project finish date. It is equal to the difference between the early start and late start (or the difference between the early finish and late finish). Also known as *slack*, *total float*, and *path float*. Free float is the amount of time an activity can slip without delaying the early start of any activity that immediately follows it.

Lag. The time delay between the start or finish of one activity and the start or finish of another activity. When expressed as a negative number, lag indicates an overlap in the activities and is also called *lead*.

Figure 10-3. Picnic at the lake: critical path.

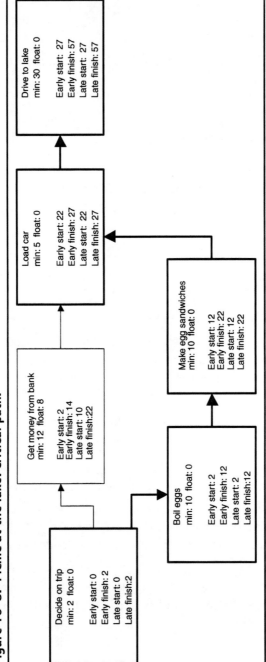

Late finish. The latest date an activity can end and still allow the project to be completed on time.

Late start. The latest date an activity can begin and still allow the project to be completed on time.

APPLICATION EXERCISE

In Chapter 9, you prepared a network diagram for your current project. Referring to that diagram, calculate the early start and finish and the late start and finish for each activity. Highlight the critical path.

APPLICATION QUESTION

Why do all activities on the critical path have zero float?

❖ ❖ ❖

CHAPTER 11

PREPARING SCHEDULES

After you have prepared the network diagram and identified the critical path identified, you are ready to prepare schedules by following two simple steps:

1. Create the initial schedule using the early start and early finish times. If necessary, you can adjust the schedule later to the late start and late finish times to account for the availability of resources. In other words, if the necessary resources are not available on the early start date, the project manager can determine to begin the activity on the late start date.

2. Assign a calendar date to the beginning of the first activity and convert the time durations on each activity to a calendar date. Alternatively, you may assign a calendar date to the completion of the project and work backward to the beginning of the project.

If the schedule shows the project will complete before the requested date, keep this extra time (float) at the end of the project to allow recovery options if the schedule slips during the life of the project. The project manager owns the float and should not give it away indiscriminately. The manager uses float to compensate for estimating variability or unforeseen problems. Team members should not be allowed to use float at their discretion.

The network diagram in Figure 11-1 shows the pump station example with calendar dates based on the early start and early finish times.

GANTT CHARTS

Once the schedule is developed, a bar chart is a helpful way to communicate schedule information since it provides an easy-to-read visual picture of the project activities. It can very quickly convey considerable information. Gantt charts (originally developed by Henry Gantt) are bar charts with time graduations along the horizontal axis and activities listed on separate lines down the vertical axis, making it easy to see the relationship between activities and time. The horizontal bars show the scheduled time frames for each activity. Connecting lines and arrows show dependencies. Figure 11-2 shows the example of the pump station shown as a Gantt chart.

CRASHING THE SCHEDULE

If the schedule you develop does not allow the project to complete when desired, you might have to take action to decrease the total project duration. This is known as *crashing the schedule*.

Analyze all the available options and choose those that provide the greatest compression for the lowest cost. Concentrate on the activities on the critical path. (Remember, shortening noncritical activities will not complete the project any sooner.)

Figure 11-1. Calendar dates for construction of a pump station.

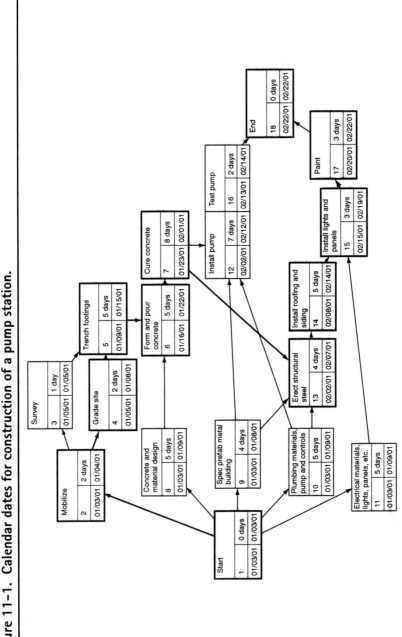

Figure 11-2. Gantt chart representation of pump station project.

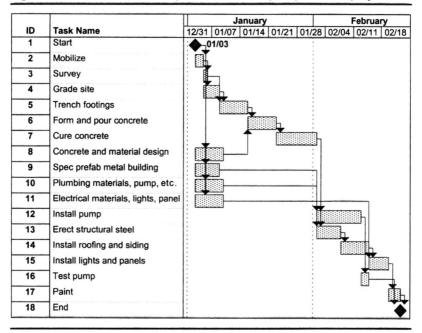

ID	Task Name	January					February		
		12/31	01/07	01/14	01/21	01/28	02/04	02/11	02/18
1	Start								
2	Mobilize								
3	Survey								
4	Grade site								
5	Trench footings								
6	Form and pour concrete								
7	Cure concrete								
8	Concrete and material design								
9	Spec prefab metal building								
10	Plumbing materials, pump, etc.								
11	Electrical materials, lights, panel								
12	Install pump								
13	Erect structural steel								
14	Install roofing and siding								
15	Install lights and panels								
16	Test pump								
17	Paint								
18	End								

Focus first on activities that occur early in the project and also those with the longest durations.

Resources

One way to crash a schedule is to change the way resources are applied to the project. The following are some options to consider:

- *Relieve employees of other responsibilities* to allow them to devote more hours each day to the project.

- *Reallocate resources from noncritical activities* to provide the extra help you need. After you reassign the resources, check to see if the critical path has shifted to include other activities.

■ *Add resources* to provide additional staff, overtime, additional equipment, vendor incentives to complete sooner, or the ability to outsource. Make wise choices because adding too many resources can cause problems in communication and interpersonal relations.

■ *Schedule overtime sparingly.* Rather than scheduling overtime in the original plan, keep it as a contingency for unforeseen problems. When using overtime, realize it is not as effective as regular work hours. Studies show that twelve hours overtime by a knowledge worker increases actual output only by the equivalent of two hours regular work. Overtime might be useful if a small increment (three to four days) will make a difference in the project, if the staff can see light at the end of the tunnel, and if extra money is an incentive to them.

Activities

Another way to crash a schedule is to change the sequence of activities or re-evaluate their estimates. The following are some options to consider:

■ *Fast track the project* by changing the sequence of activities in the network diagram to allow activities to be done in parallel (at the same time) rather than in sequence (one after another) or to allow some to overlap (for example, starting to write code on a software project before the entire design is complete). Fast tracking usually increases risk.

■ *Reconsider the accuracy of the estimates* for activities on the critical path. However, don't arbitrarily reduce the estimates to fit the time available.

Project objectives

A third way to crash a schedule is to modify the project objectives. The following are some options to consider:

- *Rethink the basic strategy* to determine better ways to accomplish the same objectives.

- *Renegotiate the project objectives.* Reduce the scope, increase the budget, or increase the time.

- *If the schedule still won't work, readdress the basic problem or opportunity* to verify that it warrants the effort it will take to complete the project.

DEFINITIONS

Crashing the schedule. Taking action to decrease the total project duration after analyzing the options to determine how to get the maximum compression for the least cost.

Fast tracking. Compressing the project schedule by changing the sequence of activities to allow activities to be done in parallel (at the same time) or to allow some to overlap.

Gantt chart. A bar chart of schedule information, typically with dates across the horizontal axis, activities listed down the vertical axis, and activity durations shown as horizontal bars under the appropriate dates.

APPLICATION EXERCISES

1. Assign calendar dates to your current project using the network diagram with critical path analysis that you completed in the previous chapter.

2. Create a Gantt chart for your current project.

APPLICATION QUESTIONS

1. To communicate project information, when would you use network diagrams and when would you use Gantt charts?

2. What are some options in crashing a schedule? What are the trade-offs in the various options? Which options are most appropriate for your current project?

CHAPTER 12

PREPARING RESOURCE PLANS

The best project plan in the world cannot be accomplished without the right people, materials, and equipment at the right place at the right time. This chapter explains how to assign the right resources when and where they are needed.

Consider the following principles when assigning resources:

- Schedules are meaningless unless the right resources are available when the activity is scheduled to begin.

- If you cannot get the right resources at the right time, you may need to replan. Do not assign the wrong person to the job just because no one else is available at that time.

- Assign scarce resources to activities on the critical path first.

- Obtain firm commitments from team members, functional managers, and senior management. Once commitments are made, the committed hours no longer belong to the function, but to the project.

■ Too few people on a project cannot solve the problems; too many people can create more problems than they solve.

■ Balance critical resources by adjusting schedules where there is float. If the activity was scheduled to begin on the early start date, try adjusting it to the late start date to see if the appropriate resources are available at that time. Meet with functional sections to level the workload as much as possible to keep in-house resources busy and to use preferred outside resources as much as possible.

■ It may be necessary to increase the project duration to get the right resources at the right times.

The following steps may be helpful in allocating resources. Although the steps refer specifically to allocating people, the same process can be followed for allocating equipment, materials, and other nonhuman resources.

IDENTIFYING THE REQUIRED SKILLS

Identify the skills required for each activity as identified on the activity estimate sheets. Also note the skill level required. You don't want to assign an entry-level editor to do a job specified for a senior editor. Likewise, you usually would not assign a senior (and higher paid) editor to do a job that could be accomplished by an entry-level editor.

RECRUITING PERSONNEL

Recruit individuals who best meet the skill requirements that were identified during the creation of the work breakdown structure. Plot each person (or group of people) and the skill requirements on a responsibility assignment matrix such as the one shown in Figure 12-1.

ASSIGNING PEOPLE TO ACTIVITIES

Assign the most appropriate people to each activity. A useful tool for determining the availability of resources is a resource histogram (Figure 12-2), which may be prepared for an individual or as a composite of a group of people with a similar skill set.

On the resource histogram, block out time needed for the following:

- *Administrative activities* (such as time cards, personnel meetings, breaks, personal leave, and sick leave).

- *Operational support* (such as training classes, coordination meetings, internal consulting, answering phone calls, travel, research, problem solving, crisis management, and other activities needed to maintain the operation).

- *Project work*—the days and hours the person (or other resource, such as equipment) is committed to project activities.

Figure 12–1. Responsibility assignment matrix.

	Skill requirement			
Person	*Technical writing*	*Proof-reading*	*Layout design*	*Customer relations*
Joe Brady	√			
Mary Fox				√
Bill Jones	√	√		
Sue Bird			√	

Figure 12-2. Resource histogram.

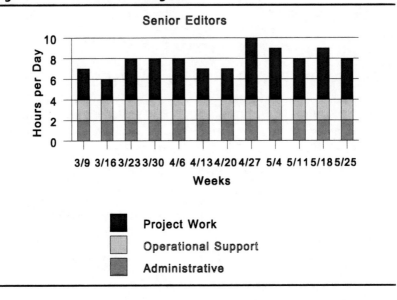

Schedules often fail because administrative and operational activities are underestimated. When this happens, fewer hours than expected can be devoted to project work.

LEVELING THE RESOURCES

When a person or other resource is over committed (such as on weeks beginning 4/27, 5/4, and 5/18 in Figure 12-2), try to level the workload using one or more of the following options.

Resources. Reallocate other available personnel or resources to provide assistance or as a replacement. Authorize overtime.

Activities. When float is available, use it to shift the schedules by using the late start rather than the early start times. Use float to extend the activity duration. (For example, rather than committing a person 100 percent for two days, use her 50 percent for four days.)

Project objectives. Reduce the scope of the activity, if possible, by approaching the activity in a different way.

As you allocate resources, it is important to consider the trade-offs in time, cost, and resources. For example, putting more employees on a particular project may get the job done faster, but may be less efficient. As Figure 12-3 illustrates, one employee can complete the job in twenty days working full time, whereas it would require forty-two days if she worked half time. (Working half time wastes a couple of days stopping and starting project work each day.) Two employees can complete the job in thirteen days and three can do it in ten days. There is no straight-line correlation between the number of employees and the days to complete the project because adding more employees means they have to expend extra time to coordinate their work. The total cost of the project increases as you add more employees: one employee half time would cost twenty-one days' work

Figure 12-3. Trade-offs in time, cost, and resources.

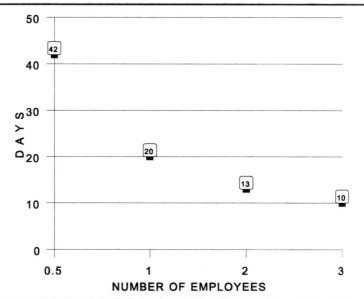

(working ½ day for 42 calendar days), one employee full time would cost twenty days' work, two employees would cost twenty-six days' work (2 × 13), and three would cost thirty days' work (3 × 10).

Allocate more employees if time is critical and fewer employees if resources are critical. In the example above, one employee is the most cost-effective choice, but three employees could complete the job most quickly if time is critical.

Some activities may take a given amount of time regardless of the number of people involved. For example, a woman can have a baby in nine months, but two women cannot do it in four and a half months.

ADJUSTING THE PROJECT SCHEDULE

Finally, adjust the project schedule based on the availability of the right resources at the right time. Leveling the workload often results in increasing the total project duration.

DEFINITIONS

Resource histogram. A chart showing the commitment of resources over a period of time.

Resource leveling. Taking action to minimize the peaks when resources are over allocated.

Responsibility Assignment Matrix. A chart that relates skill requirements to people (or groups of people).

APPLICATION EXERCISES

1. Select two activities in your current project and identify the skills required by the people who will work on each of those activities.

2. Prepare a resource histogram for each person.

APPLICATION QUESTIONS

1. What options for leveling the workload would be appropriate in your project?

2. What are the trade-offs in choosing one option over another?

❖ ❖ ❖
CHAPTER 13

PREPARING BUDGET PLANS

Budgeting is the process of allocating the cost estimates to work items to establish a cost baseline for measuring project performance. Small projects may not need extensive budget plans if you use in-house resources. Larger projects may require extensive budget plans, including basic spreadsheets, cumulative spreadsheets, and cost line graphs.

To prepare a simple budget plan, do the following:

- Total the personnel costs from each activity estimate sheet.

- Total the direct costs from each activity estimate sheet. Remember to include project management and other operational costs.

- Total indirect (overhead) costs if your organization requires they be included in your budget.

- Calculate cumulative costs.

- Determine when expenditures will be made to calculate the cash flow needed. Cash flow is usually planned according to a time interval (daily, weekly, or monthly, depending on the size and length of the project).

■ Prepare tables, charts, or graphs for each activity, for each functional section, and for the project as a whole.

The result is a project cost baseline, which is a time-phased budget that will be used to measure performance as the project progresses. It is developed by summing the cost estimates by time period and is often displayed in the form of an S-curve, as illustrated in Figure 13-1.

The following pages show examples of budget plans and graphs.

The basic spreadsheet in Figure 13-2 shows the amount of money planned for each category. As the project progresses, the actual amounts are entered and the variance calculated.

The cumulative spreadsheet in Figure 13-3 shows the cumulative costs to date and the anticipated total cost at the completion of the project.

The cumulative cost line graph in Figure 13-4 shows the cumulative actual costs to date (dashed line) compared with the

Figure 13-1. Project cost baseline.

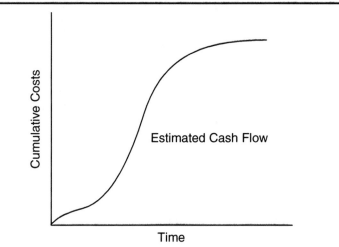

Figure 13-2. Basic cost spreadsheet.

Cost categories	January			February		
	Plan	Actual	Variance	Plan	Actual	Variance
Select demo site	$5,000			$0		
Prepare demo	$7,000			$9,000		
Conduct demo	$0			$7,500		
Evaluate demo	$0			$0		
Prepare final report	$0			$0		
Other	$200			$200		
Total direct labor	**$12,200**			**$16,700**		
Materials, etc.	$8,000			$9,500		
Total direct costs	**$8,000**			**$9,500**		
Project mgmt. support	$5,000			$5,000		
Other	$550			$550		
Total operational costs	**$5,550**			**$5,550**		
Total Project Costs	**$25,750**			**$31,750**		

Figure 13-3. Cumulative cost spreadsheet.

Cost categories	Cumulative costs to date			Anticipated total at completion		
	Plan	Actual	Var.	Plan	Actual	Var.
Select demo site	$15,000	$14,500	$500	$15,000	$14,500	$500
Prepare demo	$17,000	$17,500	($500)	$17,000	$17,500	($500)
Conduct demo	$8,500	$9,000	($500)	$9,500	$10,000	($500)
Evaluate demo	$1,500	$50	$1,450	$2,000	$2,000	$0
Prepare final report	$750	$0	$750	$750		$750
Other	$1,275	$750	$525	$2,500	$2,500	$0
Total direct labor	**$44,025**	**$41,800**	**$2,225**	**$46,750**	**$46,500**	**$250**
Materials, etc.	$8,000	$8,025	($25)	$10,000	$10,500	($500)
Total direct costs	**$8,000**	**$8,025**	**($25)**	**$10,000**	**$10,500**	**($500)**
Project mgmt. support	$12,500	$12,500	$0	$15,000	$15,000	$0
Other	$350	$325	$25	$550	$550	$0
Total operational costs	**$12,850**	**$12,825**	**$25**	**$15,550**	**$15,550**	**$0**
Total Project Costs	**$64,875**	**$62,650**	**$2,225**	**$72,300**	**$72,550**	**($250)**

Figure 13-4. Cumulative cost line graph.

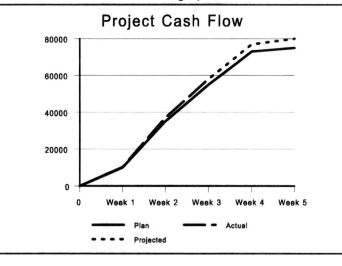

cumulative planned costs (solid line). It also shows the projected future costs (dotted line). This example shows that actual expenses to date are more than was planned. Furthermore, it anticipates that future costs will exceed the planned costs even more.

DEFINITIONS

Budgeting. The process of allocating the cost estimates to work items to establish a cost baseline for measuring project performance.

APPLICATION EXERCISES

1. Prepare a cost spreadsheet for at least one activity in your project.

2. Prepare a cumulative cost spreadsheet for the same activity.

3. Prepare a cumulative cost line graph for the same activity.

CHAPTER 14

GETTING APPROVALS AND COMPILING A PROJECT CHARTER

Now that detailed planning has been completed, compare the final schedules, cost plans, and project specifications with the original project objectives. Where there are discrepancies, you will need to negotiate adjustments and get final approvals and commitment from the customer, client, senior management, functional managers, and the project team.

This chapter details these steps, as well as the creation of a project charter—a document (or collection of documents) that formally recognizes a project and states the project approvals by the client or senior management and the authority granted to the project manager. It explains what the customer expects from the project, defines where the project begins and ends, and establishes the factors critical to the success of the project.

RECONCILING THE PROJECT OBJECTIVES

Compare the final schedules, cost plans, and project specifications with the original project objectives (see Figure 14-1).

If the project plans show the time, cost, or scope is more than the original project objectives are able to support, now is the time to negotiate any final adjustments.

- *Internal adjustments.* Negotiate revised estimates with the project team, find a different approach to complete the project, increase personnel, schedule shift work, run some activities in parallel, or take more risks.
- *External negotiations.* Renegotiate the basic project objectives with the client.

In many projects, a core piece gives 80 percent of the value of the project. Once you identify that, you may be able to reduce

Figure 14-1. Comparison of final vs. original project objectives.

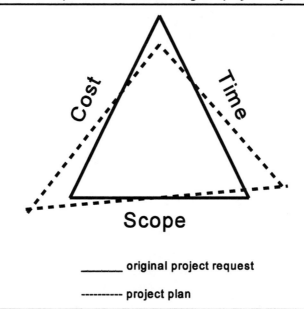

_____ **original project request**

--------- **project plan**

the size of the project by trimming back the additional pieces that give only marginal value. For example, a project to build a bridge may consist of the bridge (80 percent of the cost) and the support to the bridge (20 percent of the cost), such as toll booths, approach ramps, signs, landscaping, parkways, etc. You may be able to reduce or eliminate some of these support elements and still maintain the functionality of the bridge. However, be careful not to eliminate critical pieces of the project, such as the approach ramps.

GETTING APPROVALS AND COMMITMENTS

Get written approvals from the customer, client, senior management, functional managers, and project team. Get everything in writing. Unless it's on paper, it has not been said. Over time, people may forget the conditions attached to a promise and only remember the promise.

Determine what the commitments mean. To what lengths will the person go to meet the project objectives? What will happen if other work conflicts with commitments to this project? What support will senior management give the project? What do you expect from them? Do they understand the expectations the same way you do?

Get the appropriation of budgets, personnel, equipment, and other resources.

CREATE A PROJECT CHARTER

Compile a project charter, including at least the following:

 Purpose of the project, including the business need the project addresses

- Scope statement, including project objectives of time and cost
- Description of the final product or service the project will create
- Statement of the authority of the project manager to apply resources to project activities
- Schedules, budgets, and other project plans prepared in the previous steps

It is important that these documents be formalized in writing and kept in a single binder or Web site so that they are accessible to all members of the project team, the client, and the customer. The project charter is a dynamic document that is updated and refined as needed. However, any changes in project objectives, schedules, or budgets must be controlled through a formal change process (see Chapter 19). When such changes are approved, the project charter must be updated.

DEFINITIONS

Project charter. A set of documents that states the purpose and requirements of the project, including approvals by the client or senior management and the authority of the project manager to expend resources.

APPLICATION EXERCISE

1. List the items that would be included in a charter for your current project.
2. Explain where the documents would be kept and how they would be made available to all interested parties.

APPLICATION QUESTION

1. How can a project charter help you manage projects better?

❖❖❖
CHAPTER
15

SETTING UP A MONITORING AND CONTROL PROCESS

Control is the process of comparing actual performance to the plan to determine the variances, evaluate possible alternatives, and take appropriate corrective action.

The ability to control a project is directly tied to the effectiveness of the project plan. You need a plan to tell you where you are supposed to be and you need status information to tell you where you are. Even with the best of planning, problems will still occur but they will be fewer and less serious. This chapter explains how to set up a monitoring and control process you can use throughout the life of the project.

PRINCIPLES OF MONITORING AND CONTROL

■ Establish a formal process to control changes in the project (see Chapter 19). Revise project plans as needed to keep them realistic and accurate, but only allow them to be revised by those who are authorized.

■ Don't micro-manage the project. Let functional managers and line supervisors develop for their own use a set of subactivities, cost plans, and detailed checklists to help them accomplish their activities.

■ Elevate problems to the lowest level of management that can make the decision and take action. Never present a problem without a recommended solution (or two). Otherwise, management may come up with an inappropriate solution or never give you a decision.

■ Be sure that schedule progress, cost expenditures, and scope performance are calculated and reported using methods consistent with the way the plan was established.

■ If you manage several projects at once, you may wish to rank them so you can handle regular-schedule projects differently from fast-track-schedule projects.

    A. *Significant, highly-visible projects.* They require more monitoring.

    B. *Average projects.* They require average monitoring.

    C. *Low priority projects.* They require less monitoring.

ESTABLISHING A PLAN TO MONITOR AND CONTROL THE PROJECT

Before the project begins, the project manager should consult with the project team, the customer, and the client to determine the information needs, data collection methods, and frequency of data collection.

Determining Information Needs

The project manager determines what information is needed to control the project. If the needed information is not collected, the project cannot be controlled. Gathering information that is not needed is a waste of effort.

To control the project, the project manager compares the current status with the plan to determine variances. Since the project objectives were specified in terms of time, cost, and scope, it is helpful to collect status information in the same terms. Suggestions for specific information to collect about the time, cost, and scope can be found in the following chapters.

Determining Data Collection Methods

The project manager determines how project status information will be collected.

Electronic

Electronic data collection can be quick and cost-effective. When team members have access to a computerized system, they can input status information directly into the computer and it is immediately accessible by the project manager and others. Electronic systems can share information, so information need be entered only once. For example, work hours entered by team members can update project cost reports and also be transmitted directly to the finance department for payroll.

Although electronic data collection is preferred by many, it is not recommended unless:

- The organization operates consistently under sound project management principles.
- The project team members have been trained in project management concepts and methods.
- The project team has the skills and discipline to report correct data consistently.

Manual

If the organization lacks the maturity described above, manual data collection methods may be preferred. These consist of traditional methods of paper time cards and status reports.

Onsite Inspections

The project manager gathers additional information by conducting scheduled and unscheduled onsite inspections. In addition to what the numbers say, the project manager needs to see firsthand how well the team works together and if there are conflicts or other factors influencing performance.

One-on-One Interviews

A face-to-face interview is an effective way to gather information. In this setting, team members can give their opinions, suggestions, and critiques of the work.

Team Meetings

Although a meeting can be used to collect project information, is usually not an efficient use of team members' time. However, it is important that the team meet together occasionally to confirm that the data collected matches the perspectives of the team as a whole. This is especially appropriate when the team completes a milestone event or a major phase of the project. With team synergy, issues may surface that would not come to light in any other way. Team meetings are also helpful for brainstorming, coordinating work, building team spirit and comradery, group decision making, and achieving group consensus.

Determining Frequency of Data Collection

The project manager establishes an update cycle for various types of data. This cycle may be immediate (data is entered when an event happens), daily, twice a week, weekly, twice monthly, monthly, or quarterly.

Issues to consider when determining frequency may include:

- The requirements and expectations of the client.
- The average duration of the project activities. (For example, if most activities are scheduled to last a day or two, a weekly update cycle would not be frequent enough.)
- Experience. (For example, in dealing with unknown personnel or subject matter, it may be appropriate to collect data more often for early problem identification.)

STATUS INFORMATION

Once project work begins, the project manager systematically collects status information according to the methods and frequency previously determined. When status information is collected, the project manager compares it with the schedule, budgets, and scope identified in the project plan to determine the variances. A variance exists when the actual status does not equal the planned status.

VARIANCES

Not all variances have a negative impact on the project and not all variances deserve corrective action. The project manager analyzes any variance to determine:

- The impact of the variance on the project
- Whether the impact is a problem
- The cause of the variance, including reasons and the people involved

■ Whether the cause of the variance will create variances elsewhere in the project

REPORTS

Prepare and publish reports that show:

■ What the plan says should be happening
■ What is actually happening (status)
■ Variance between the plan and the status

COURSE OF ACTION

The project manager develops and analyzes solutions to the problem. If the project manager has sufficient authority, she decides on a course of action. If not, she takes recommendations to the level of management that can make that decision.

Taking action includes the following steps:

■ Implement the decision.
■ Follow up to be sure the action solves the problem.
■ Take additional action if necessary to solve the problem.
■ Document the decisions that make significant changes in approved project plans.
■ Take preventive action to be sure similar problems do not happen. (For example, double-check other estimates or analyze procedures.)

APPLICATION EXERCISE

Develop a written plan for monitoring your current project. Determine the information needs, data collection methods, and frequency.

APPLICATION QUESTIONS

1. Consider a potential problem that could occur in your current project. What recommendation would you make to solve the problem and to whom would you make it?

2. What alternatives would you suggest if they don't accept your recommendation?

CASE STUDY ❖❖❖❖❖❖❖❖❖

Urgent Care Hospital

Urgent Care Hospital has recently received several large grants to modernize and upgrade the care they provide to the community. The hospital has determined to spend some of the money to upgrade the radiology department and has hired you to manage a project to install a new CAT scanner (computerized axial tomography scanner) to provide better care to critical patients.

The new CAT scanner will require a major renovation of the radiology department, which is estimated to take eight weeks. Although the head of the department is eager to have the new machinery, she is not happy about the disruption the construction will cause. The scanner is expected to arrive March 1 and will take three weeks to install. The construction renovation cannot begin until after the installation is complete. The four operators who will use the new equipment also need two weeks of training.

The estimated costs are as follows:

Purchase:	$1,000,000
Installation:	$45,000
Operator training:	$16,000
Renovation:	$96,000

Since the hospital expects to generate income of $50,000 a month on the new scanner, its managers are anxious to begin using it as soon as possible with the least possible disruption to hospital functions. The head of the radiology department has come to you asking you to reduce the total project time as much as possible. She feels that thirteen weeks is too long of a disruption.

To accommodate the request, you now need to complete the following tasks:

■ Determine what can be done to "crash the schedule."

■ Prepare a network diagram and assign calendar dates to each activity.

■ Determine what resources are needed for each activity.

■ Prepare a cash flow report showing the projected expenditures for each week of the project.

(Suggested answers are given in Appendix A at the back of the book.)

EXECUTING THE PROJECT

SECTION OBJECTIVES

- Learn the steps of project monitoring and control.

- Understand the methods of controlling the project schedule, cost, and scope.

- Discover how to report project information effectively in order to support corrective actions.

❖❖❖
CHAPTER 16

INITIATING THE PROJECT

KICKOFF MEETING

You can start a project on the right foot by holding a formal kickoff meeting with the client, customers, project team members, and other stakeholders. This is a great opportunity to define the roles and responsibilities of everyone present and communicate the project plans clearly and concisely. It is the first step in establishing a team identity and building comradery.

On large projects, you may wish to build team spirit and identity by developing a project logo or slogan to use on letterhead, project reports, and even t-shirts and mugs.

COMMUNICATING PROJECT PLANS

Be sure to communicate project information to all stakeholders: the project team, functional managers, senior management, customers, and the client.

Present the appropriate level of detail to each group. Management may be interested in summary-level information whereas team members need much more detail. Be sure to cover all areas of planning, including:

- Statement of the project objectives
- Work breakdown structure
- Logic network diagrams
- Schedules for individual activities and the project as a whole
- Charts showing estimated costs and projected cash flow
- Resource histograms

APPLICATION QUESTIONS

1. In your current project, which project plans would you communicate to the client, customers, and team members?
2. What level of detail would you provide to each?

❖❖❖
CHAPTER 17

CONTROLLING PROJECT OBJECTIVES

Logic network diagrams, schedules, and budget plans are not just planning tools that are archived once planning is completed. They are used regularly in controlling the project throughout its life. This chapter explains how to use project plans, together with status information you collect as the project progresses, to control time, cost, scope, and resources.

TIME CONTROL

Time control is the process of comparing actual schedule performance to the baseline schedule to determine variances, evaluate possible alternatives, and take the appropriate action. To effectively control time, be sure the schedule plans are in sufficient detail to adequately control the activities.

Actions

Consider the following actions to control time:

- *Systematically collect schedule performance data,* including the following:
  Actual start time of each activity
  Estimated remaining duration of activities in process
  Actual finish time of each activity
  Changes in time estimates
  New activities that have been identified
  Previously planned activities that are no longer needed

- *Compare this status information with the baseline schedule.*

- *Analyze variances to determine their impact.* Variances can be positive or negative. The activity may have taken three days too long, or it may have been completed three days early. Not all variances have a negative impact on the project and some variances are so small they don't deserve corrective action. Also try to determine the cause of the variance so you can take corrective action, where needed, to prevent it from happening again.

- *Prepare and publish reports.* See Chapter 18 for ideas on reporting, including example time control reports.

- *Determine a course of action.* If you determine the variance warrants action, determine what that action will be.

- *Take corrective action.* Act on schedule deviations quickly, especially in the early stages of the project where the tone of the entire project is set.

Delays often happen near the conclusion of a project as workers scramble to complete extra tasks identified during the course of the project. Hence the following humorous adage: "The first 90 percent of the project takes the first 90 percent of the time; the other 10 percent of the project takes the other 90 percent of the time."

COST CONTROL

Cost control is the process of comparing actual expenditures to the baseline cost plans to determine variances, evaluate possible alternatives, and take appropriate action. To effectively control costs, be sure cost plans are prepared with sufficient detail.

Actions

Consider the following actions to control costs:

- *Systematically collect cost performance data,* including the following:
  Labor hours expended
  Estimated remaining labor hours needed to complete activities
  Percentage complete of activities in process
  Nonlabor expenditures to date
  Estimated remaining nonlabor expenditures needed to complete activities
  Funds committed but not paid and dates when these obligations must be paid
  New activities that have been identified
  Previously planned activities that are no longer needed

- *Compare expenditures* to the baseline cost plans.

- *Analyze variances* to determine their impact. Cost variances can be positive or negative. The activity may have cost more or less than budgeted. Not all variances have a negative impact on the project and some variances are so small they don't deserve corrective action. Also try to determine the cause of the variance so you can take corrective action, where needed, to prevent it from happening again.

■ *Prepare and publish reports.* See the next chapter for ideas on reporting, including example cost control reports.

■ *Determine course of action.* If you determine the variance warrants action, determine what that action will be.

■ *Take corrective action.* Act on cost overruns in a timely manner, especially in the early stages of the project where the tone of the entire project is set.

Be aware that expenditures may escalate near the end of a project to cover labor and purchases that had not been anticipated.

Common Causes of Cost Problems

Since costs can be a major source of frustration in a project, it is helpful to have a good understanding of where costs can get out of control. Consider the following list of common causes:

■ Poor budgeting practices, such as (1) basing the estimates on vague information from similar projects rather than the detailed specifications of the project at hand, (2) failure to plan sufficient contingency budget, (3) failure to correctly estimate research and development activities, or (4) failure to consider the effects of inflation on the cost of materials or labor.

■ Receiving or analyzing status information too late to take corrective action.

■ A climate that does not support open and honest disclosure of information.

■ Indiscriminate use of the contingency budget by activities who overrun their budgeted cost.

■ Failure to rebudget when (1) flaws are discovered, (2) technical performance falls below performance standards, or (3) changes in project scope are approved. During the course of the project, many small decisions are made that ultimately impact costs. For example, when engineering decides on the final design of a product feature, conventional accounting reports may not show the impact of these design decisions on production costs. In that case, the project manager must make sure that the cost impact is known before such decisions are made.

Avoiding Common Cost Problems

You can avoid such cost problems by following good estimating and budgeting practices, as described in earlier chapters. Careful monitoring and quick corrective action will also help keep cost problems to a minimum. If you find yourself in budget trouble, you may be able to recover by focusing on critical activities. Many projects have certain activities that consume a great percentage of the total cost of the project. With the aid of a detailed cost breakdown and current information on costs committed, you may be able to make adjustments in these key activities to contain costs.

SCOPE AND QUALITY CONTROL

The scope document includes not only a description of the features and functions of the product or service but also quality measures (such as technical specifications, performance requirements, quality standards, safety regulations, security issues, and environmental considerations). These measurements are used regularly in controlling quality once the project begins. To effectively manage scope, quality standards must be defined in the project scope statement in quantifiable terms that can be measured and reported. Scope management is interested in both the management of the project work and the quality of the product or service that is created by the project.

Scope and quality control is the process of comparing actual performance to the scope statement to determine variances, evaluate possible alternatives, and take the appropriate action. As you do so, consider the following issues:

■ Scope and quality may be more difficult to measure and control than time or cost.

■ The more complex the project, the more control the worker has over quality because managers may not have the technical expertise to recognize good or poor quality.

■ When workers are up against tight time and cost restrictions, they may tend to cut corners on scope and the quality of the final product suffers. In these cases, the project manager needs to pay particular attention to scope.

Actions

Consider the following actions to control scope and quality:

■ *Systematically collect performance data.*
Are the specifications being met as identified in the scope statement?
Are the quality standards being met as identified in the scope statement?

■ *Compare performance to the scope statement.*

■ *Analyze variances to determine their impact.* Variances can be positive or negative. The finished product may not meet the specifications or it may exceed them. Not all variances have a negative impact on the project and some variances are so small they don't deserve corrective action. Also try to determine the cause of the variance so you can take corrective action, where needed, to prevent it from happening again.

■ *Prepare and publish reports* that detail where the project is meeting, not meeting or exceeding project specifications.

■ *Determine a course of action.* If you determine the variance warrants action, determine what that action will be.

■ *Take corrective action.* Act on scope deviations quickly, especially in the early stages of the project where the tone of the entire project is set.

Although quality is the responsibility of everyone on the project team, there should also be a quality management function within the project team to ensure that all aspects of the project satisfy the quality standards.

RESOURCE CONTROL

The project manager must maintain control over all resources used in a project. Although nonhuman resources may be controlled easily, human resources may be more difficult to manage.

Resource control is the process of comparing actual performance to the resource plans to determine variances, evaluate possible alternatives, and take the appropriate action.

A project is in control at the macro level only when all team members are in control of their own work at the micro level. Rather than micromanaging team members, the project manager sets up an environment wherein team members can control their own work.

Actions

■ Be sure that all team members understand the basic objectives of the project and know how their tasks contribute to the project as a whole.

- Have team members prepare individual plans for accomplishing their work.

- Ensure that team members have the appropriate skills and resources to do the job.

- Empower team members to accomplish their tasks by giving appropriate authority and information. Also provide supervision and performance feedback.

If team members practice proper control, then weekly reports can just serve as checks and balances.

CONTROL THRESHOLDS

Consider again the example of an aircraft flight plan presented in Chapter 8. The pilot's flight plan (see Figure 17-1) allows a range rather than a fixed course. As long as the pilot stays within the 8-mile-wide band, he is within the accepted tolerance limits, and is considered "in control." By comparison, a project manager determines the ranges in schedule, budget, and scope that are acceptable variances from the plan. Should the project manager report and take action on a schedule variance of one day? Or two days? Should he take action if the team spends $100 over the planned cash flow for the week? Or $1,000? Or $10,000?

Some projects can be more tightly controlled than others. Work that can be measured accurately can be controlled with

Figure 17-1. Range limits for an aircraft flight plan.

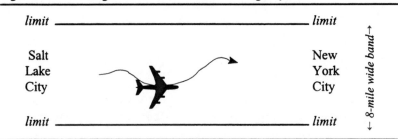

tighter tolerances. Work that is less precise (such as research or knowledge work) must be allowed greater tolerances.

TOOLS TO USE IN CONTROLLING PROJECT OBJECTIVES

A variety of tools and techniques may be used to determine whether work is being accomplished according to the quality level and specifications defined in the project planning stage. Some of the more typical methods are discussed in the following section.

Inspection

Inspection includes measuring, examining, and testing— performed to determine whether the results conform to predefined specifications. Inspections should be performed on individual activities and also on the final product of the project. A variety of inspection forms and checklists may be developed to allow information to be collected quickly and in a standardized format.

Statistical Sampling

Because it is not always possible or practical to inspect every activity or every item produced, principles of statistical sampling may be applied to ensure that inspection results are reliable. For example, you can choose to inspect ten activities at random out of the total one hundred activities. Principles of statistical sampling and probability must be used to determine the number of items out of the total that must be inspected in order to apply those results to the total with reasonable accuracy. A great body of literature is available on appropriate sampling techniques.

Flowcharting

Flowcharts can provide useful information about process flow and may be helpful to analyze how problems occur. It may be sufficient to have a general top-down flowchart that shows the major steps in the process (see Figure 17-2). If more specific information is needed, a detailed flowchart may be created to show each process step, including decision points and feedback loops.

Control Charts

Control charts are graphs that display periodic results along with established control limits. They are used to determine if a process is in control or in need of adjustment. Control charting helps to distinguish between normal variations that are to be expected and unusual variations produced by special causes that need to be identified and corrected. The sample control chart in Figure 17-3 shows the average daily rejections in a production facility for two weeks.

Control limits identify the natural variation that occurs in the process. In the example, if the production facility had established an upper control limit of 8 and a lower control limit of 3.5, all the points in this two-week period would be within the normal and expected variation except the rejection rate of 8.3 on Day Six. Points outside the control limits generally signal that something has occurred that requires attention, such as a problem with equipment, defective materials, or an employee. In addition, the *rule of seven* indicates that when seven or more points in a row occur on the same side of the mean, or when they tend in the same direction—even though they may be within the control limits—they should be investigated. It is extremely unlikely that seven points in a row would be on the same side of the mean if the process is in control.

Figure 17-2. Flowchart of publications process.

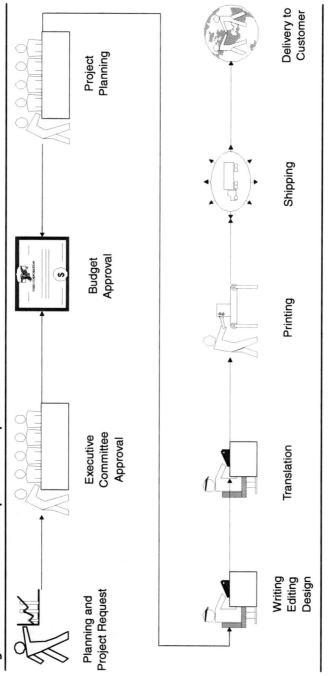

Planning and
Project Request

Executive
Committee
Approval

Budget
Approval

Project
Planning

Writing
Editing
Design

Translation

Printing

Shipping

Delivery to
Customer

Figure 17-3. Sample control chart.

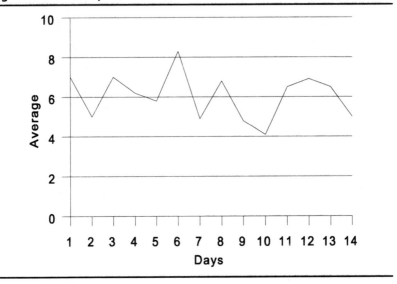

Trend Analysis

Trend analysis uses mathematical techniques to forecast future outcomes based on historical results. Line graphs, pie charts, bar charts, and histograms may be used to identify trends and to focus on controlling the influencing factors (see Figure 17-4).

Pareto Diagrams

The Pareto Principle states that a few vital elements (20 percent) account for the majority (80 percent) of the problems. For example, in a manufacturing facility, 20 percent of the equipment problems may account for 80 percent of manufacturing down time. Therefore, it would be advantageous to identify and focus on correcting that 20 percent of the equipment problems. A Pareto diagram (see Figure 17-5) may be used to focus attention on the most critical issues. It is a bar chart with elements arranged in descending order of importance, generally by magnitude of frequency, cost, or time.

Figure 17-4. Sample graphs for a printing facility.

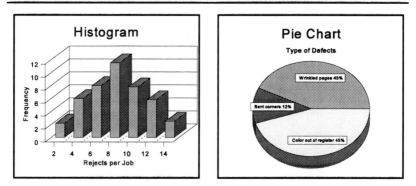

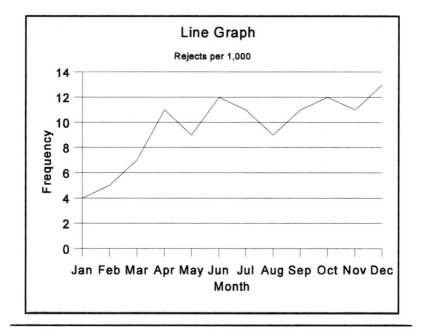

Cause-and-Effect Diagrams

A cause-and-effect diagram is a graphical representation of the relationships that exist between factors (see Figure 17-6). It can be used to explore a wide variety of factors and how they relate to factors that may cause them. Also called a fish bone diagram,

Figure 17-5. Pareto diagram.

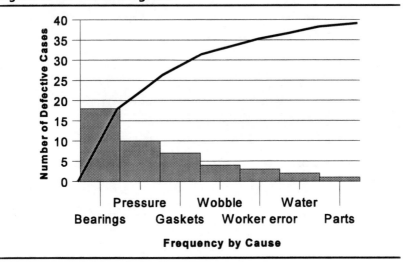

Figure 17-6. Cause-and-effect diagram.

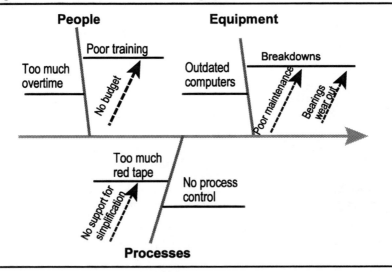

it is a useful tool in brainstorming, planning activities, and examining processes.

Earned Value Analysis

Earned value analysis (also known as variance analysis) is a way to measure and evaluate project performance. It compares the amount of work planned with what is actually accomplished to determine whether the project is on track.

Earned value analysis, which was developed in the 1960s to allow government agencies to determine when a contractor should receive progress payments for work, is a helpful tool for monitoring and controlling projects. It uses various calculations and ratios to measure and report on the status and effectiveness of project work.

Although earned value calculations are usually done by computer, it is important to know the basis of each calculation and understand what they mean.

The first step in earned value analysis is to determine the following three key values:

1. *Planned Value* (PV) is the planned cost of work scheduled to be done in a given time period. The amount of PV is determined by totaling the cost estimates for the activities scheduled to be completed in the time period. Planned Value is also called the *Budgeted Cost of Work Scheduled* (BCWS).

2. *Earned Value* (EV) is the planned cost of work actually performed in a given time period. This is a measure of the dollar value of the work actually performed. The amount of EV is determined by totaling the cost estimates for the activities that were actually completed in the time period. Earned Value is also called the *Budgeted Cost of Work Performed* (BCWP).

3. *Actual Cost* (AC) is the cost incurred to complete the work that

was actually performed in a given time period. The amount of AC is determined by totaling the expenditures for the work performed in the given time period. It should include only the types of costs included in the budget. For example, if indirect costs were not included in the budget, they should not be included in AC calculations. Actual Cost is also called the *Actual Cost of Work Performed* (ACWP).

Once these values are determined, you can use them in various combinations to provide measures of whether work is being accomplished as planned. For example:

Schedule Variance. Schedule variance is determined by subtracting the earned value from the planned value. This calculation measures the difference between the planned and the actual work completed. A positive result means the project is ahead of schedule; a negative result means the project is behind schedule.

$$SV = EV - PV$$

Cost Variance. Cost variance is determined by subtracting the earned value from the actual cost. It measures the difference between the planned (budgeted) cost and the actual cost of work completed. A positive result means the project is under budget; a negative result means the project is over budget.

$$CV = EV - AC$$

Once these calculations are made, various indices or ratios can be used to evaluate the status and effectiveness of project work. These efficiency indicators provide valuable information that can be used to control the project. The two most commonly used indices are the schedule performance index and the cost performance index.

1. *Schedule Performance Index.* This is a ratio of work performed to work scheduled. The index is calculated by dividing the earned value by the planned value. This ratio is a measure of efficiency in the schedule. A value less than 1 means the project has accomplished less than planned and is behind schedule; a value greater than 1 means the project is ahead of schedule. Analyzing the SPI several times during the project provides an indication of how the project is performing compared to the project plan. This index may also be used to forecast the project completion date.

$$SPI = EV / PV$$

2. *Cost Performance Index.* This is a ratio of budgeted costs to actual costs. This index is calculated by dividing the earned value by the actual cost. This ratio is a measure of cost efficiency (how efficiently dollars are being spent). A value less than 1 means the work is costing more than planned; a value greater than 1 means the work is being produced for less than planned. For example, a CPI of .67 means that for each $1.00 spent on the project, we produce $0.67 worth of value. Analyzing the CPI several times during the project provides an indication of the project's direction concerning costs.

$$CPI = EV / AC$$

These indices provide a quick snapshot of the project's efficiencies at a given point in time. However, they are more valuable when used periodically during the life of the project to track trends and take corrective action. They also provide an element used in the following calculations to forecast the completion of the project:

Budget at Completion (BAC) is the estimated total cost of the project when completed. It is calculated by totaling the cost of all activities outlined on the work breakdown structure.

Estimate to Complete. This is the expected additional cost needed to complete the project. It is calculated by subtracting the budgeted cost of work performed from the earned value, then dividing the result by the cost performance index. This estimate shows the expected additional cost needed to finish the project, including adjustments to the BAC based on project performance to date.

$$ETC = (BAC - EV) / CPI$$

Estimate at Completion. This is the expected total cost of the project when completed. It is calculated by adding the actual cost and the estimate to complete. This estimate includes adjustments to the BAC based on performance to date.

$$EAC = AC + ETC$$

DEFINITIONS

Cause-and-effect diagram. A graphical representation of the relationships that exist between factors. Used to explore a wide variety of factors and their relationships to factors that may cause them. Also called a fish bone diagram.

Control charts. Graphs that display periodic results along with established control limits. They are used to determine if a process is in control or in need of adjustment.

Cost control. The process of comparing actual expenditures to the baseline cost plans to determine variances, evaluate possible alternatives, and take the appropriate action.

Earned value analysis. A method of measuring and evaluating project performance. It compares the amount of work planned with what is actually accomplished to determine whether the project is on track. Earned value analysis is also known as variance analysis.

Flowchart. A quality control tool that provides information about process flow.

Pareto diagram. A bar chart with elements arranged in descending order of importance, generally by magnitude of frequency, cost, or time. Used to focus attention on the most critical issues.

Pareto Principle. A vital few elements (20 percent) account for the majority (80 percent) of the problems.

Resource control. The process of comparing actual performance to the resource plans to determine variances, evaluate possible alternatives, and take the appropriate action.

Rule of seven. A rule of thumb in control charting that indicates that when seven or more points in a row occur on the same side of the mean, or when they tend in the same direction—even though they may be within the control limits—they should be investigated.

Scope control. The process of comparing actual performance to the scope statement to determine variances, evaluate possible alternatives, and take the appropriate action.

Time control. The process of comparing actual schedule performance to the baseline schedule to determine variances, evaluate possible alternatives, and take the appropriate action.

Trend analysis. Using mathematical techniques to forecast future outcomes based on historical results.

APPLICATION EXERCISES

1. Develop a plan to control time on your current project. Specify what data you will collect and how.

2. Determine how you will control costs on your current project. Review the common causes of cost problems and explain how you will avoid these errors.

3. Write down a plan for controlling scope on your current project. Explain how you will ensure that workers maintain high quality.

4. Plan how to control resources on your current project. List the specific actions you will take.

5. To be sure you understand the concepts of earned value, read the following example and perform the calculations:

The Dunbar Project was scheduled to cost $1,500 and was originally scheduled to be completed today. As of today, however, the project has spent $1,350 and it is estimated that only two-thirds of the work has been completed..

Calculate the schedule and cost variances and the schedule and cost indices.

(The answers are given in Appendix A at the back of the book.)

CHAPTER 18

REPORTING ON PROJECT OBJECTIVES

Project managers spend much time preparing reports, but often they exert too little effort to determine what information needs to be communicated to whom. Reports should be designed to communicate exactly what needs to be communicated. Because projects are approved based on the objectives of time, cost, and scope, it makes sense to focus reports on the same three aspects.

This chapter discusses issues to consider as you prepare and publish reports, and then provides samples of various kinds of reports.

REPORTING CONSIDERATIONS

As you prepare reports, use the following guidelines:

- Maintain concise, top-quality project plans and status reports. Be sure everything you publish is accurate.

■ Keep all stakeholders appropriately informed, including team members, customers, clients, functional managers, and senior management. Determine for each audience what information they need to perform their functions and design reports accordingly. Keep them informed—but not over-informed—with the information they need to make decisions and take corrective action.

■ Use exception reporting by including only major variations from the plan. Stakeholders don't have time to digest pages and pages of project information, and there is little need to report on items where status matches the plans. Use software programs to analyze project information and report on variances from the project plans.

■ Establish problem-reporting thresholds. Determine how significant a variation from the plan needs to be before you report on it. For example, establish thresholds for how many dollars over budget or how many days late.

■ Choose the best format for the report, such as a table, line graph, histogram, or bar or Gantt chart.

■ On each report, clearly state the purpose of the report and the action to be taken.

GRAPHICAL REPORTS

It is important to make reports easy to read. The first step is to be sure reports contain only the information needed by the recipient. Next, determine whether the reports can be further simplified by converting data to graphics. This is particularly useful in summary reports sent to upper management. A simple pie chart or line graph may be much easier to interpret than a page full of text or numbers.

Some reports use the symbol of a traffic signal as a visual indicator of project status (see Figure 18-1). Green means the project is on track, yellow indicates minor trouble, and red

Figure 18-1. Traffic signal as indicator of project status.

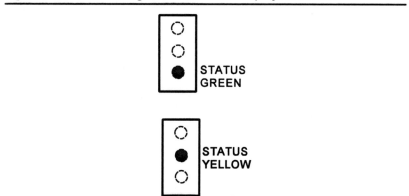

warns of major trouble. The project manager establishes the thresholds for each project. For example, green may indicate less than 5 percent variance from the plan, yellow could be a variance of 5 percent to 10 percent, and red indicates any variance over 10 percent.

REPORTING PERCENT COMPLETE

Planning and reporting on percent complete is particularly useful when one part of the activity is more difficult than another part. Consider the construction of a brick wall (see Figure 18-2). What happened? Did the workers slack off as the days went by? Actually, the construction plan was faulty because it specified laying 100 bricks per day, with the unstated assumption that it takes the same effort to lay each of the 1,000 bricks. To assume this—and to measure and report it as such—is misleading. As you can see from our example, the workers laid more bricks per day in the early days of the project and fewer bricks per day toward the end of the project, because the higher rows of bricks required scaffolding and additional time to move materials up and down. This should have been considered by the project team in the original estimates and the project should have been planned accordingly.

Figure 18-2. Construction of a brick wall: plan vs. actual.

Specifications:
    1,000 total bricks
    20 bricks wide by 50 bricks high

Construction plan:
    lay 100 bricks per day
    for 10 days

Actual performance:

Day	Bricks laid
1	139
2	131
3	127
4	119
5	113
6	98
7	85
8	76
9	61
10	51

The theory of percent complete provides a more accurate way of planning and reporting on an activity where one part of the activity is more difficult than another. Rather than measuring and reporting on the number of bricks laid, this method measures and reports the percent complete. A report of "629 bricks laid of the total 1,000 bricks at Day 5" may be misleading to those who don't understand how the project was planned. A report of "Job 50 percent complete at Day 5" is clear.

SAMPLE REPORTS

Status Report

The status report in Figure 18-3 is highly graphical and presents a lot of information quickly. It was designed to report summary

Figure 18-3. Sample status report.

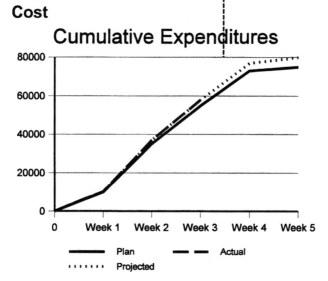

Status Report: 1 June

Schedule (6 months to complete)

| Mar | Apr | May | Jun | Jul |

Cost

Cumulative Expenditures

80000

60000

40000

20000

0

0   Week 1   Week 2   Week 3   Week 4   Week 5

———— Plan   — — Actual

• • • • • • • Projected

Scope

	Status to date	Status at completion
Quality standards	ok	ok
Legal requirements	ok	anticipate delays
Zoning variance	ok	ok

information to upper management on the three aspects of the project objectives: schedule, cost, and scope.

Schedule information is presented on a single timeline with a solid arrow above the line indicating performance to date (in the example, positioned at the end of the first week of May). A quick visual comparison with the dashed vertical line indicating the date of the report (1 June) tells the recipient of the report that the project is running three weeks late (the difference between the end of the first week of May and 1 June). The solid horizontal bar shows the scheduled length of the project. In this example, the project is scheduled to be completed at the end of June. However, the dashed line and arrow indicates that the expected completion date has been extended to the end of July. Therefore, although the project is only three weeks late as of the date of the report, additional delays are anticipated such that the project is expected to complete four weeks late (at the end of July rather than at the end of June).

Cost information is presented next in a chart showing cumulative project expenditures. The dashed line shows that actual expenditures to date are more than was planned. Furthermore, the dotted line shows a projection to overspend even more before the project is completed.

Scope identifies a few key indicators, which are listed with a simple "ok" or a warning of potential problems.

Schedule Baseline Plan

The Gantt chart in Figure 18-4 shows the baseline plan for a software demonstration project. The activities are shown as gray bars. The black bars represent a summary of the activities in each phase of the project. The lines show dependencies between the activities. This is the baseline schedule plan distributed to everyone involved in the project.

Figure 18-4. Schedule baseline plan: Gantt chart.

ID	Task Name	Feb	Mar	Apr	May	Jun	Jul	Aug	Sep	Oct	Nov	Dec	Jan	Feb	Mar	Apr	May	Jun	Jul	Aug	Sep	Oct	Nov	Dec	Jan
1	**Select Demonstration Site**																								
2	Identify possible sites																								
3	Evaluate sites																								
4	Select site																								
5	**Prepare for Demonstration Site**																								
6	Develop plan																								
7	Approve plan																								
8	**Conduct Demonstration**																								
9	Conduct demonstration																								
10	**Evaluate Demonstration Results**																								
11	Prepare evaluation plan																								
12	Collect data																								
13	Analyze data																								
14	Determine recommendations																								
15	**Prepare Project Report**																								
16	Prepare report																								
17	Review and approve report																								

Schedule Status Report

Because everyone involved with the project is familiar with the baseline plan, a project manager may decide to use the same chart to monitor and report on progress throughout the life of the project (see Figure 18-5). As activities are completed, solid lines are drawn through the gray activity bars and actual start and finish dates appear in the appropriate columns.

Summary Schedule Status Report

The chart in Figure 18-6 is identical to the chart in Figure 18-5 except the individual activities have been removed, leaving only the summary steps. This report is sent to recipients who only require summary information. It is also called a milestone schedule.

Cost Report

The simple spreadsheet in Figure 18-7 lists the same steps as the previous schedule reports, but provides financial data (rather than schedule data) for a given period.

Cumulative Cost Report

The spreadsheet in Figure 18-8 is similar to the cost report but shows cumulative costs to date and the anticipated total costs at the completion of the project.

Cumulative Cost Line Graph

The report in Figure 18-9 shows the same information as the previous report, but in graphical form.

(text continues on page 182)

Figure 18–5. Schedule status report.

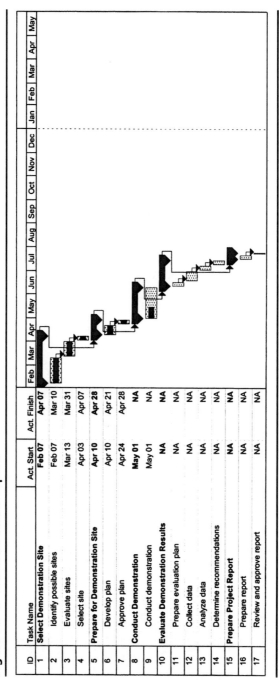

ID	Task Name	Act. Start	Act. Finish
1	**Select Demonstration Site**	Feb 07	Apr 07
2	Identify possible sites	Feb 07	Mar 10
3	Evaluate sites	Mar 13	Mar 31
4	Select site	Apr 03	Apr 07
5	**Prepare for Demonstration Site**	Apr 10	Apr 28
6	Develop plan	Apr 10	Apr 21
7	Approve plan	Apr 24	Apr 28
8	**Conduct Demonstration**	May 01	NA
9	Conduct demonstration	May 01	NA
10	**Evaluate Demonstration Results**	NA	NA
11	Prepare evaluation plan	NA	NA
12	Collect data	NA	NA
13	Analyze data	NA	NA
14	Determine recommendations	NA	NA
15	**Prepare Project Report**	NA	NA
16	Prepare report	NA	NA
17	Review and approve report	NA	NA

Figure 18-6. Summary schedule status report.

ID	Task Name	Act. Start	Act. Finish	Feb	Mar	Apr	May	Jun	Jul	Aug	Sep	Oct	Nov
1	Select Demonstration Site	Feb 07	Apr 07										
2	Prepare for Demonstration Site	Apr 10	Apr 28										
3	Conduct Demonstration	May 01	NA										
4	Evaluate Demonstration Results	NA	NA										
5	Prepare Project Report	NA	NA										

Figure 18-7. Sample cost report.

	January			February		
Cost categories	Plan	Actual	Variance	Plan	Actual	Variance
Select demo site	$5,000			$0		
Prepare demo	$7,000			$9,000		
Conduct demo	$0			$7,500		
Evaluate demo	$0			$0		
Prepare final report	$0			$0		
Other	$200			$200		
Total direct labor	**$12,200**			**$16,700**		
Materials, etc.	$8,000			$9,500		
Total direct costs	**$8,000**			**$9,500**		
Project mgmt. support	$5,000			$5,000		
Other	$550			$550		
Total operational costs	**$5,550**			**$5,550**		
Total Project Costs	**$25,750**			**$31,750**		

Figure 18-8. Cumulative cost report.

	Cumulative costs to date			Anticipated total at completion		
Cost categories	Plan	Actual	Var.	Plan	Actual	Var.
Select demo site	$15,000	$14,500	$500	$15,000	$14,500	$500
Prepare demo	$17,000	$17,500	($500)	$17,000	$17,500	($500)
Conduct demo	$8,500	$9,000	($500)	$9,500	$10,000	($500)
Evaluate demo	$1,500	$50	$1,450	$2,000	$2,000	$0
Prepare final report	$750	$0	$750	$750		$750
Other	$1,275	$750	$525	$2,500	$2,500	$0
Total direct labor	**$44,025**	**$41,800**	**$2,225**	**$46,750**	**$46,500**	**$250**
Materials, etc.	$8,000	$8,025	($25)	$12,700	$17,950	($5,250)
Total direct costs	**$8,000**	**$8,025**	**($25)**	**$12,700**	**$17,950**	**($5,250)**
Project mgmt. support	$12,500	$12,500	$0	$15,000	$15,000	$0
Other	$350	$325	$25	$550	$550	$0
Total operational costs	**$12,850**	**$12,825**	**$25**	**$15,550**	**$15,550**	**$0**
Total Project Costs	**$64,875**	**$62,650**	**$2,225**	**$75,000**	**$80,000**	**($5,000)**

Figure 18-9. Cumulative cost line graph.

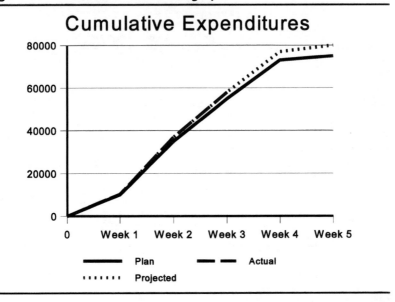

Instructions on Reports

Reports are most helpful when they clearly explain the purpose of the report and the action requested. Consider the report in Figure 18-10 from one company division to another.

DEFINITIONS

Exception report. A report that shows only major deviations from the project plan, rather than all deviations.

Percent complete. A method of reporting where the amount of work completed on an activity is expressed as a percent of the total work required for the activity.

APPLICATION EXERCISE

Review the reports you use in your current project. Using the suggestions in this chapter, determine how you can revise the reports to make them more useful.

Figure 18–10. Sample report instructions.

To: Europe Translation Division
From: Headquarters Production Control
Date: 15 December 2004
Re: Resubmission of Translations in French

According to the central tracking system, the following manuals have been translated but not yet received in the production division for graphics production.

Please submit these jobs to us at your earliest convenience so they may be processed without delay.

Item #	Language	Title	Date Translation Completed
52206	French	PRT Software Manual	14 Jan 04
31596	German	T5 Software Screens	13 Mar 04
52206	Spanish	PRT Software Manual	10 Mar 04

❖❖❖
CHAPTER 19

CONTROLLING CHANGES IN THE PROJECT

During the course of a project, circumstances may come to light that necessitate minor or major adjustments to the plan. Not all changes are bad, yet not all changes can be made once a project is underway and after time, cost, and scope have been established.

Frequent scope changes may be an indication of inadequate up-front planning. They most often occur because of errors or omissions in the planning stage. Frequent changes may also be an indication of weak management in the organization, or a sign that the organization is trying to handle more work than it has resources available. Changes may also be brought on by external events, such as changes in government regulations, new technologies, or adding new products or competitors.

It is important to put in place a formal change control process to handle proposed changes to the plan. The system should include processes for submitting, evaluating, approving, and communicating changes in the project plan. However, don't make the system more complex than it needs to be. A lack of control can mean chaos, whereas an excessive amount of red tape can be overly burdensome to the project. Large projects with high visibility or a great degree of risk deserve a more rigorous change control process.

Change control is necessary to manage the potential effects on the project budget, schedule, and scope. Remember that the project triangle must be kept in balance. Changes in the time, cost, or scope of the project must be accompanied by appropriate changes in at least one other side of the triangle. After the project is underway, the client may decide he wants new features added to the product, but he may still expect it to come in on the original schedule and budget. Change control can protect the project from "scope creep" (the tendency for scope to increase during the course of the project without proportionate increases in time or cost). Change control is sometimes called configuration management.

Actions

- ■ Establish processes for submitting, evaluating, approving, and communicating changes in the project plan, including changes in time, cost, or scope. Define tolerance guidelines so team members know which minor changes they can accept and which changes must go through the formal change control process.

- ■ Review change requests with the project team. Consider the impact of the change on all aspects of the project. Determine the added value the change represents for the client, customer, or project team. Identify the causes of the change and determine if these causes necessitate changes in other areas of the project or in future projects.

- ■ Study alternative courses of action and determine their effect on the project.

■ Approve or reject changes, or provide alternative solutions.

■ Communicate approved changes to all concerned.

■ Document and track all changes, reporting on their effect on the project.

Change Request and Approval Form

The form in Figure 19-1 illustrates the kind of information needed to control change requests. Develop an appropriate form to use with your project.

Change Control Log

A change control log (see Figure 19-2) also may be used by the project manager to document and track changes. Such a form helps:

■ Keep track of changes.

■ Determine why changes are made.

■ Justify changes to management.

■ Capture lessons learned for future projects.

DEFINITIONS

Change control. A formal process to manage proposed changes to the project plan. Includes processes for submitting, evaluating, approving, and communicating changes. Sometimes called configuration management.

APPLICATION EXERCISE

Define the change control process for your current project. Specify the processes to be followed and the forms to be used.

Figure 19-1. Project change request and approval form.

Project title: Software Demo	Date: 8/30/2004
Activity # 15	**Revision #** 1

Activity description:
Set-up demonstration equipment

Submitted by:	Date:

Description of request for change:
Since this activity was originally estimated, new equipment has become available that can greatly increase the effectiveness of the software demo. Senior management requests that we use the new equipment. The demo staff also prefers the new equipment.

Reason for change:
The new equipment was not considered in the original project plan because it was not available at that time. This new equipment should be considered for all future demo projects.

Impact of change on this activity and other activities

Activity	Impact on schedule	Impact on cost	Impact on scope
#15 s/w demo	No impact.	New equipment costs $500 more than old equipment.	Better quality demo; not more difficult to operate.
#13 site preparation	2 additional hours to install cables; can complete the same day.	Increase of $100.	Change in specifications to allow additional cables.

Approvals

Project Manager:	Date:
Activity Owner:	Date:
Functional Manager:	Date:
Senior Manager:	Date:

Figure 19-2. Change control log.

#	Date of change request	Description of change and business reason	Impact on schedule, resources, and risk	Decision (date, by whom)
1	9/20/04	New equipment for software demo. New equipment became available after the demo project was planned.	Cost increased $600; better quality demo; no schedule impact.	Approved 9/22/04 by Bob Tagg.
2				
3				

CHAPTER 20

CONDUCTING PROJECT
EVALUATIONS

To ensure project success, you need periodic project evaluations to be sure work is being accomplished as planned. Even though you constantly collect data about costs, schedules, and work accomplished, you should plan specific reviews as a chance to step back and take a good look at the project to be sure that everything is progressing as it should.

A project is like a journey, and project plans (such as work breakdown structures, schedules, and cost reports) serve as road maps to help team members measure their precise location. Project reviews are checkpoints along the way to ensure the project is on course. If the project has deviated from course, the review can identify the variance and help you make the proper adjustments.

Project reviews also help to motivate team members, customers, and clients. The evaluations provide feedback to help everyone stay focused on the project objectives. People work best when they know how they are progressing toward the goal.

Feedback helps people stay committed and motivated. People thrive on constructive feedback.

WHEN TO PERFORM PROJECT EVALUATIONS

Project work should be evaluated in four general ways: on-going reviews, periodic inspections, milestone evaluations, and final project audit.

On-Going Reviews

Work on the project should be reviewed constantly by project team members as part of an on-going quality assurance program. Even though others may inspect for quality at specified checkpoints, the responsibility for quality rests with individual workers. They must feel a commitment to produce quality work—even if no one were to inspect it! Quality must be incorporated into the project from the beginning. It cannot be inspected in later.

On-going reviews should ensure that the standards included in the project scope statement are being applied to the work. Such standards may include safety regulations, security issues, licensing requirements, environmental considerations, and legal requirements. On-going reviews should also ensure that finances are being handled according to guidelines and that other project data, such as schedule data, are being reported correctly.

Periodic Inspections

Team leaders, functional supervisors, or quality inspectors should review project work periodically to ensure that project objectives are being met. These may be daily, weekly, or monthly inspections according to the needs of the project. Since it is generally not feasible to inspect every bit of work produced, it should be determined at the beginning of the project what will be inspected at what frequency.

Milestone Evaluations

Additional project evaluations should take place when milestone events are reached, for example, at the conclusion of each major phase of the project. Such an evaluation is used to certify that all work scheduled to be accomplished on that phase of the project has been completed according to specifications.

Final Project Audit

A final audit should be made at the conclusion of the project to verify that everything was completed as agreed to by the client, customer, and project team. This audit provides information that may be used in project closure and acceptance. This is also a time to gather and document lessons learned during the project. What was done well? What could be improved? What could be learned from this project to help on future projects?

CONSIDERATIONS IN PROJECT EVALUATIONS

Each of these four types of project evaluation should consider quality of work, team performance, and project status.

Quality of Work

Each evaluation should review the work performed to ensure it is according to specifications. The project charter contains the project scope and quality specifications that should be met. The audit should determine whether proper quality has been maintained, or whether quality has been compromised to meet schedule and cost objectives.

Team Performance

Sports teams review game films periodically to evaluate their performance and see where they need to improve. Without this kind of review, they may become very good at playing badly. Project teams also need to evaluate whether they are performing as well as they can. Such reviews may be conducted by the project team members themselves, by the project manager, or by an independent auditor.

Comparison with Past Performance

If consistent data is gathered over time, periodic reviews provide a history to which current performance may be compared. This comparison over time shows whether team performance is improving or declining.

Comparison with Benchmarks

Team performance may also be compared with that of other companies or industry standards. Benchmarking is the process of defining a standard or point of reference to measure quality or performance. A survey of comparable companies showing their performance or quality levels could be used as a reference point in evaluating your project. If the industry standard to construct a comparable building is $75 per square foot, you could measure your results against that to see if you are doing as well as the industry average.

Project Status

The project status review compares the planned with actual results and notes the variances. It reports on any deviations in the schedule, cost, scope, or performance, or whether such appear to be likely in the future.

Special attention should be given to activities on the critical path, because any delay in these activities will cause the project to be late (unless, of course, subsequent activities are completed in less than the scheduled time). Also give special review to activities with high risk. Early identification and mitigation of problems can minimize their impact on your project.

DEFINITIONS

Benchmarking. The process of defining a standard or point of reference to measure quality or performance.

APPLICATION QUESTIONS

1. Does your organization have a formal evaluation process? What project reviews do you currently perform?

2. What improvements could you make in evaluating performance, quality, or status?

✦✦✦
CHAPTER 21

MANAGING RISK

Risks are uncertain events or conditions that, if they occur, have a positive or negative effect on the project objectives. All projects have a certain degree of risk that needs to be managed. The project manager determines where risks are likely to affect the project, makes contingency plans for them, and responds to them when they occur.

This chapter describes the risk management processes of identifying, analyzing, and responding to project risk. The purpose of risk management is to maximize the results of positive events and minimize the results of adverse events.

IDENTIFYING RISK

The first step in developing a risk management plan is to identify the potential risk events.

Consider Possible Sources

The chart in Figure 21-1 identifies the major categories of risk and gives common examples of each.

Figure 21-1. Major categories of risk.

Risk category	Examples
Technical	New breakthroughs, design errors or omissions
Administrative	Processes, procedures, changes in roles or responsibilities
Environmental	Culture of the organization, change in management or priorities, office politics
Financial	Budget cuts, cash flow problems, corporate unprofitability, unchecked expenditures, changing economic conditions
Resource availability	Specialized skills or critical equipment not available
Human	Human error, poor worker performance, personality conflicts, communication breakdown
Logistical	Inability to deliver materials to work face-to-face
Governmental	Government regulations
Market	Product fails in the marketplace, consumer expectations change, new competitor products

Determine Likely Risks

To identify potential risks, simply ask yourself "What could go wrong?" Review the work breakdown structure for the project, the cost estimates, and resource plans and consider what might happen that could cause any aspect of the project to deviate from the plans. Define specific risk events and describe what specifically might go wrong. For example, ground-breaking may be delayed because of legal problems in securing the building permit. Describe the effect of each potential event. Identify what would cause the risk event to happen (often called triggers) and describe any conditions or signs that may warn you of the impending event.

Consider both internal and external events that could effect the project. Internal events are things under the control of the project team, such as work assignments or cost estimates. External events are things beyond the influence of the project team, such as technology shifts or changing economic conditions.

We typically think of risk as a negative event that would cause harm or loss to the project. However, risk events can also include opportunities with positive outcomes. A change in economic conditions may increase the available labor force and allow you to hire more workers to complete the project sooner. Although a potentially positive outcome, you need to assess the impact on the project schedule and cost plans and determine your course of action.

You can never anticipate all possible risks, nor should you expend the effort to try to identify every conceivable problem. Simply identify those that are fairly likely. The cost of prevention should never exceed the cost of impact should the potential problems actually occur!

Conduct Ongoing Risk Identification

Risk identification is not a one-time event. Economic, organizational, and other factors will change during the course of the project that may bring to light additional sources of risk. Risk identification should first be accomplished at the outset of the project, then be updated on a regular basis throughout the life of the project.

ASSESSING RISK

Once you have identified the potential risk events to be included in the plan, the next step is to estimate the probability of occurrence and determine the impact if the event were to occur.

You may wish to give greater analysis to potential risks associated with activities on the critical path, since a delay in these activities is more likely to delay the final outcome of the project.

Also give attention to points in the network where activities converge, because these tend to have a greater degree of risk.

For each potential risk event, estimate its impact on the time, cost, and scope of the project. Remember that a single risk event could have multiple effects. For example, the late delivery of a key component could cause schedule delays, cost overruns, and a lower-quality product.

To help prioritize the potential risks, you may wish to plot them on a chart, such as the one shown in Figure 21-2, to help you determine which risks are most critical.

Focus primarily on risks with high impact and a high ability to influence, (the top-right quadrant). These are critical risks that you can do something about, either in preventing them from happening or in responding to their impact when they do happen. In a highway construction project, potential equipment breakdowns may be one such risk. The impact is great because construction stops when there is no functioning equipment. In such situations you have high ability to influence the potential risks by using reliable equipment and having good preventive maintenance plans.

Secondly, focus on risks with high impact but low ability to influence (the top-left quadrant). In our example of a highway

Figure 21-2. Prioritizing potential risks.

I	High impact; Low ability to influence	High impact; High ability to influence
M		
P		
A	Low impact; Low ability to influence	Low impact; High ability to influence
C		
T		

ABILITY TO INFLUENCE

construction project, such a risk may be the threat of a union strike over a requested pay raise. Such a potential risk has great impact because it would halt construction. Since you have little control over whether the union calls a strike, you must delegate this potential problem to company management and union representatives. Contingency plans should be made for these types of risks because of their high impact.

Of lesser priority are the risk events that fall in the bottom two quadrants because their impact on the project is low. An example of a risk that may appear in the bottom-right quadrant (low impact but high ability to influence) is late delivery of trees and bushes for landscaping along the roadside. The impact is low because traffic can begin using the highway even if the landscaping is not yet completed. Your contingency plan may be to have an alternate vendor in place, ready to deliver the trees and bushes if the primary vendor fails.

Finally, consider the potential risk events in the bottom-left quadrant (low impact and low ability to influence). An example of such a risk may be the late arrival of permanent signs for the highway. If the signs are manufactured in a state facility, you may not be able to choose another vendor. However, the impact is low because you can continue to use the temporary signs until the permanent ones are installed.

RESPONDING TO RISK

The purpose of risk response is to minimize the probability and consequences of negative events and maximize the probability and consequences of positive events.

Planning Responses

A response plan should be developed before the risk event occurs. Then, if the event should occur, you simply execute the plan already developed. Planning ahead allows you the time to carefully analyze the various options and determine the best course of action, so you aren't forced to make a quick and perhaps not-well-thought-out response to a threatening situation.

Possible Responses

In developing a response plan, consider ways to avoid the risk, transfer it to someone else, mitigate it, or simply accept it.

Avoiding

It may be possible to eliminate the cause, and therefore, prevent the risk from happening. This may involve an alternative strategy for completing the project. For example, rather than assigning work to a new, less expensive contractor, you may choose to reduce the risk of failure by using a known and trusted contractor even though the cost may be higher. You can never avoid all risk, but you can try to eliminate as many possible causes as possible.

Transferring

It may also be possible to transfer some risk to a third party, usually for the payment of a risk premium. For example, you can avoid the chance of a cost overrun on a specific activity by writing a fixed-price contract. In such a case, the contractor agrees to complete the job for a predetermined (higher) price and assumes the potential consequences of risk events. If the risk is low, you could choose to accept the risk and write a cost-plus contract, paying the contractor only the actual costs plus a predetermined profit. Other examples of risk transference include the purchase of insurance, bonds, guarantees, and warranties.

Mitigating

Mitigation plans are steps taken to lower the probability of the risk event happening or reduce the impact should it occur. For example, you can reduce the likelihood of a product failure by using proven technology rather than "cutting-edge" technology. Mitigation costs should be appropriate to the likelihood of the risk event and its potential impact on the project. Some mitigation strategies may not take a lot of effort, but may have large pay-offs in eliminating the potential for disaster. On a project with a tight deadline, the risk of delayed delivery of raw materials may be disastrous. If two vendors can provide materials at essentially the same price, but one has a much larger inventory and a significantly better history of on-time delivery, choosing the vendor with the better track record may be an easy mitigation strategy with a potentially large pay-off.

Accepting

When there is a low likelihood of a risk event, when the potential impact on the project is low, or when he cost of mitigation is high, a satisfactory response may be to accept the risk. For example, midway into a project to reengineer a manufacturing plant to increase its efficiency and output, the economy moves into a recession. The company chooses to proceed with the project anyway and accept the risk that lower sales may reduce the return on investment below what was expected.

Response Plan Outcomes

After considering the options of avoiding, transferring, mitigating, or accepting the risk, the outcome of response planning is a risk management plan, contingency plans, and reserves. The risk management plan documents the procedures that will be used to manage risk throughout the project. It lists potential risk events, the conditions or signs that may warn you of the impending event, and the specific actions to be taken in response. Contingency plans describe the actions to be taken if a risk event should occur. Reserves are provisions in the project plan to mitigate the impact of risk events. These are usually in the form of contingency reserves (funds to cover unplanned costs), schedule reserves (extra time to apply to schedule overruns), or management reserves (funds held by general management to be applied to projects that overrun).

RESPONDING TO RISK

The project manager and other team members monitor the project throughout its life, looking for triggers and signs that may warn of impending risk events. When risk events happen, they take the corrective action identified in the risk management plan.

When an unplanned risk event occurs, a response must be developed and implemented. This is often called a workaround. After the response is implemented, the risk management plan should be reviewed and updated if necessary. It may also be necessary to adjust other project plans or the basic project objectives.

As changes in the project occur, it may be necessary to repeat the steps of identifying risk, assessing risk, and planning responses to risk.

DEFINITIONS

Contingency plan. A plan that describes the actions to be taken if a risk event should occur.

Mitigation plans. Steps taken to lower the probability of the risk event happening or reduce the impact should it occur.

Reserves. Provisions in the project plan to mitigate the impact of risk events. Usually in the form of contingency reserves (funds to cover unplanned costs), schedule reserves (extra time to apply to schedule overruns), or management reserves (funds held by general management to apply to projects that overrun).

Risk management. The process of identifying possible risks, making preventive and contingency plans, and executing those plans when risk events occur.

Risk management plan. A plan that documents the procedures that will be used to manage risk throughout the project.

Trigger. An occurrence or condition that causes an event to happen.

Workaround. The response to an unplanned risk event.

APPLICATION EXERCISE

Evaluate your organization's ability to manage risk and explain what you can do to improve the way you manage the risk in projects.

CLOSING THE PROJECT

A good project management methodology includes formal steps to close the project. The purpose of project closure is to verify that all work has been accomplished as agreed and that the client or customer accepts the final product. This is often called *scope verification*. The steps involved in project closure ensure that all payments are made and finances reconciled. Project documentation and final reports are completed and any remaining budget, materials, or other resources are properly dispersed.

Project closure is also a time to recognize individual efforts and celebrate project success. Typically, employee evaluations, vendor evaluations, and customer satisfaction reviews are completed at this time as well. The project manager ensures that team members have a smooth transition to other projects or work assignments.

In large projects, many of these actions may be appropriate at the end of each phase of the project as well as at the conclusion of the entire project.

The checklist in Figure 22-1 gives further detail on items you may need to consider in the project closeout.

Figure 22-1. Project closure checklist.

		Check here when completed
Project		
1	Have all activities in the project plan been completed?	
2	Have all work orders been completed?	
3	Have all contracts been completed?	
4	Have all outstanding commitments been resolved?	
5	Has the client or customer accepted the final products?	
6	Are all deliverables completed?	
7	Has agreement been reached with the client on the disposition of any remaining deliverables?	
8	Have external certifications and authorizations been signed and approved?	
9	Have all audits been completed and issues resolved?	
10	Have ongoing maintenance procedures been activated?	
Finances		
11	Have all payments been made to vendors and contractors?	
12	Have all costs been charged to the project?	
13	Have project accounts been closed?	
14	Have remaining project funds been returned?	
Project documentation		
15	Have project plans and supporting documentation been revised to reflect the "as-built" condition?	
16	Have final project reports been prepared and distributed?	
17	Has the project plan been archived with all supporting data?	

18	Have "lessons learned" been documented, shared with appropriate prople, and archived with the project plans?	
Personnel		
19	Are all parties aware of the pending closeout?	
20	Has effort been recognized and rewarded?	
21	Have project personnel been reassigned?	
Resources		
22	Has excess project material been dealt with?	
23	Have project facilities, equipment, and other resources been reallocated?	

DEFINITIONS

Project closure. Formal steps taken at the conclusion of a project to get acceptance of the final product, close project records, and reallocate personnel and other resources.

Scope verification. Verifying that all project deliverables have been accomplished as agreed.

APPLICATION EXERCISE

Consider how you closed your previous projects. Explain what you will do at the end of your current project to make project closure more effective.

CASE STUDY ❖❖❖❖❖❖❖❖❖

Western Power

To respond to growth in southern California, Western Power decided to build an innovative, $1 billion power plant near San

Diego. The new power plant would implement new technologies not only to produce higher levels of clean power to benefit the nearby cities, but also to generate enough power to sell to other utility companies in the rest of southern California and parts of adjacent states. The executive management of Western Power was most anxious to complete the project as soon as possible because of the tremendous revenue they anticipated from the additional sales.

However, once news of the proposed power plant got out, it generated much opposition from nearby residents. As construction began, they initiated several lawsuits in an attempt to stop construction. Western Power responded with an intense public relations campaign to convince local residents of the benefits of the project.

After a few months' delay, the project got underway and the marketing department began contacting other utility companies to develop contracts for selling power. When it became apparent that income from power sales would not be as great as originally anticipated, management asked Rob Hedge, the project manager, to find ways to reduce the construction budget so the company could maintain the expected level of profitability from the new plant.

Rob couldn't find many ways to reduce construction costs because of tight regulations by environmental protection organizations and numerous other governmental agencies. Therefore, he asked the architects and engineers to see what design changes could be made to reduce costs. The architects made several suggestions that would have reduced costs substantially, but the engineers could not make the new technologies work with the suggested changes. They did agree on a few changes that were implemented immediately. Rob asked the architects and engineers to be on the construction site regularly, looking for other ways to modify the design to reduce costs.

One year into the five-year project, the president of the construction company approached the president of Western Power complaining of numerous changes that caused confusion and extra work. He explained that engineers were making on-site changes without notifying the architects to update the blueprints. Construction managers were often unaware of these changes, which meant that subsequent tasks were sometimes done in error. Also, the architects had made some unsuitable design changes without consulting the engineers, which caused rework.

Upon investigation, Western Power management learned from the regulatory agencies that two portions of the first phase of the project did not meet government standards, and would have to be rebuilt. When management also learned that the project was six months behind schedule and 10 percent over budget, it fired the project manager.

You have been hired as the new project manager. What actions would you take to remedy the problems and gain better control of this project? Consider the following in your answer:

■ Project objectives

■ Project change control

■ Risk

■ Quality, time, and cost control

■ Project justification

(Suggested answers are given in Appendix A at the back of the book.)

❖❖❖
SECTION 4

LEADING THE PROJECT TEAM

SECTION OBJECTIVE

Learn management and interaction skills
needed by project managers in such areas
as teamwork, communication, decision-
making, managing change, and managing
performance.

23

DEVELOPING PROJECT TEAMS

Successful project managers need more than just the tools of planning, scheduling, and controlling—they must be able to effectively develop and lead a project team. Whether that team is one person or a hundred people, internal employees or external contractors, the project manager must be able to turn a group of diverse people into a cohesive team. Time and again, studies reveal that projects fail when the project manager does not build a strong project team.

This chapter points out how a project manager leading a project team differs from a functional manager supervising individual workers. It also discusses the stages of growth as teams mature. Many books have been written about project teams, and project managers would be wise to learn how to lead teams successfully.

LEADERSHIP ENVIRONMENT

The team-oriented method of working today is different from the traditional hierarchical style of management. The roles of superior ("boss") and subordinate ("worker") have given way to equal adult-adult relationships. In technical fields where the worker often knows more about the job than the manager does, the equal adult-adult relationships allow responsibility to be shared, which increases quality and reduces project costs.

In a leadership environment, as opposed to a management environment, the project manager becomes a partner or facilitator with the project team to accomplish the work at hand. The project manager helps the team catch the vision of what needs to be done, then provides what the team needs to accomplish the work. Figure 23-1 illustrates the differences between management and leadership.

Figure 23-1. Differences between management and leadership.

	Management	Leadership
Organizational type	Functional	Project
Type of work	Similar work	Unique work
Worker skill level	Skilled	Higher skilled
Authority	Delegates authority	Empowers people
Organizational structure	Hierarchy	Team
Management style	Superior-subordinate; the employee "works for the boss"	Facilitated; the leader "works for the team"
Criteria for decisions	Data, policies, administrative requirements	Experience, intuition, and vision
Focus	Today	Tomorrow

One of the most important roles of a project manager is to lead the project team. A leader inspires (rather than dictates or manages) others to do things to help the organization reach its goals. A project manager who cannot lead people finds it difficult to manage a project—especially when the project team does not belong to the project manager.

TEAM DEVELOPMENT

Individuals brought together to work on a project don't automatically become a team the day the project begins. It takes time and energy to transform a group of people into a team. The individuals likely come from varied backgrounds and they may have different reasons for being involved in the project. They may represent different levels (positions) from various departments within the company, or come from other organizations altogether. There may be cultural, linguistic, religious, or social diversity among team members, and it may take time for them to get to know each other and understand each other's motivations. Even if they are all committed to the project, they will likely have different reasons for that commitment and different perspectives on what constitutes success in the project. For example, it may be difficult for managers representing information technology, purchasing, and sales to agree on the right mix of quality, cost, and schedule.

Stages of Team Development

Teams go through several stages of growth on their way to becoming a cohesive and productive team. A helpful way to understand this maturation process is to consider the four stages as forming, storming, norming, and performing. Teams typically progress through these four stages, although there may be times in the team's development when members regress to one of the previous stages, especially when dealing with complex problems.

Forming

In this initial stage, people feel excitement, anticipation, optimism, suspicion, fear, or anxiety. There is typically a level of confusion, and team members look to the team leader to provide structure as they identify the role of each member and determine how to function as a team. They also attempt to define their assigned task and decide how to accomplish it. In this stage, the project manager concentrates on providing leadership, direction, and a lot of information.

Storming

As goals and objectives are clarified, team members see the gap between reality and their initial expectations. They may experience dissatisfaction and begin to reexamine their goals and structure. They may also question the role of the team leader or other team members and become defensive or competitive. At this stage, it is critical for the project manager to keep the team focused and provide encouragement.

Norming

In this stage, team members begin to resolve conflicts through increased cooperation and trust. They settle on ground rules and boundaries and establish norms about how to work together. They rally around each other with common spirit and goals and get down to work. In this stage, the project manager provides leadership and continued encouragement.

Performing

In this final stage, team members work together productively and produce high-quality results. They prevent problems or work through them constructively. They provide their own direction and encouragement and feel satisfaction in working with the team. In this stage, the project manager can focus on getting the team the resources and recognition it needs.

APPLICATION QUESTIONS

1. What is the difference between a manager and a leader?

2. What leadership skills do you still need to work on to become a truly effective team leader? How will you do so?

3. What is the current level of development of the team on your current project?

4. What can you do to help them progress to the next stage?

MANAGING CONFLICT

Conflict is a disagreement between people caused by personality differences, miscommunication, or technical and administrative issues. If you have a heterogeneous project team—which is ideal—you will experience conflict. Conflict exists in almost any human interaction and the project manager must be prepared to deal with it. Don't try to eliminate conflict, but manage it. This chapter presents potential causes of conflict then offers suggestions on how to handle conflict.

Conflict is beneficial when it pushes people to higher levels of performance or when it results in the development of new information that enhances the decision-making process. Conflict is detrimental when it impedes project objectives with no positive consequences.

Little or no conflict decreases effectiveness in the organization. It produces apathy, stagnation, and a lack of new ideas. A high level of conflict also decreases effectiveness in the organization. It creates disruption, chaos, and a lack of cooperation. However, an optimal level of conflict increases organizational effectiveness. It produces self-evaluation and innovation.

POTENTIAL CAUSES OF CONFLICT

The chart in Figure 24-1 shows some of the major potential sources of conflict. Although conflict may emerge from many sources, it would be prudent to consider each of those sources listed to anticipate problems from those areas and think through how you would deal with each.

■ If your project is on a tight time frame, what conflicts may arise due to schedules and how will you resolve them?

■ Do you anticipate conflicts in priorities among the team members or other stakeholders?

■ If resources are scarce, how will you resolve the conflicts that will likely arise in allocating sufficient resources to get the job done?

Figure 24–1. Potential causes of conflict.

Potential cause	Characteristics
Schedules	Disagreements about the timing, sequencing, or scheduling of project activities.
Project priorities	Conflicts about the sequence of activities or the relative importance of one project over another.
Resource allocation	Disagreements about the availability, allocation, or scheduling of personnel or other resources.
Technical and performance	Disagreements about technical issues, performance specifications, technical trade-offs, and the means to achieve performance.
Administrative procedures	Conflicts about how the project is managed, such as role definition, reporting relationships, responsibilities, plans of execution, or work agreements with other groups.
Cost	Conflict over cost estimates or the allocation of funds.
Personality conflict	Disagreements about interpersonal differences. These are often ego-centered.

- Given the nature of your project, are there specific technical or performance issues that may cause conflict?

- Do you anticipate administrative conflicts and how will you work them out?

- If the budget is tight, how will you manage conflicts that may arise over the allocation of funds?

- Given the personalities of the team members assigned to your project, do you foresee any interpersonal conflicts?

Spending a few minutes thinking through these issues ahead of time may help you be more keenly aware of potential conflicts so you can identify them early and solve them quickly.

HANDLING CONFLICT

Because many people have never been taught how to sit down and work out their differences, even a small conflict may escalate into a major problem. Therefore, the project manager may need to provide training on interpersonal skills to team members.

Below are listed various methods of handing conflict, ordered from the most effective (listed first) to the least effective (listed last).

Problem Solving

This is a rational, fact-based approach where disputing parties solve their differences by focusing on the issues, looking at alternative approaches, and selecting the best alternative. Problem solving may contain some elements of compromising and smoothing. This is usually the most effective way to handle conflict. It helps the parties learn to work together to resolve differences and find solutions that are not based on emotion or power plays.

Compromising

Compromising involves bargaining and searching for solutions that bring some degree of satisfaction to the parties involved. Since compromise yields less than optimum results, the project manager must weigh such actions against program goals.

Smoothing

Smoothing seeks to maintain friendly relations by emphasizing common areas of agreement and de-emphasizing areas of difference. Although it may not address the real issues, it may be effective because identifying areas of agreement may put the disagreement in clearer perspective. Thus, project work can often continue in areas where there is agreement.

Forcing

Forcing involves a straightforward use of authority power in resolving the conflict by exerting one's viewpoint over the others. This method should be used only as a last resort or in urgent situations because it may cause resentment and deterioration of the work climate.

Withdrawing

Withdrawing means retreating from the conflict issue. In this method, the person purposely ignores the conflict because he wants to avoid causing problems, or he withdraws from it out of fear, perhaps feeling inadequate to resolve the issue. This method may be precarious because if the issue at hand is important to the other party, withdrawing or ignoring it may intensify the situation. However, it may be an appropriate strategy in situations where other methods are not effective. For example, it may be a temporary strategy to allow the other party to cool off or to buy time to study the issue further.

APPLICATION QUESTIONS

1. Identify conflict situations that have occurred in your project. What caused the conflict? How was the conflict handled? What better ways may have been used to deal with the conflict?

2. What method do you typically use to manage conflict? If you use more than one method, which have you found to be the most effective?

3. What ideas from this chapter can you implement in your current project?

25

COMMUNICATING
EFFECTIVELY

One of the most
important skills for a project manager is
the ability to communicate well. Although
effective communication is not a panacea
for all problems, it is essential in running
a successful project. When there is conflict or dissatisfaction in
the project team, it can often be traced to difficulties in communication.

Communication is a function of trust. When trust is high,
communication is effective. It is important for project teams to
communicate effectively in all forms: verbal, nonverbal, writing,
and listening. Studies show that improving communication is
perhaps the most critical improvement needed in organizations.
A written communication plan for your project can help you
focus on communication issues. This chapter discusses the process of communication and provides suggestions on improving
communication skills in the areas of listening, nonverbal communication, and focused conversation.

PROJECT COMMUNICATION PLAN

The project manager should develop a communication plan for each project. A communication plan describes what information is communicated, to whom, how, and how often. You may wish to use a communication matrix like the one shown in Figure 25-1.

As you read the remainder of this chapter, consider issues you need to incorporate into your communication plan.

THE PROCESS OF COMMUNICATION

Effective communication requires that:

- The information is transmitted properly.
- The receiver understands the communication.
- The receiver interprets the information correctly.

As illustrated in Figure 25-2, the sender determines what information to share and encodes the message. The receiver decodes the message to determine its meaning and then responds accordingly. Encoding and decoding may be affected by values,

Figure 25–1. Communication matrix.

Method	Client	Customer	Team member A	Team member B
Formal status reports	Monthly	Quarterly	Weekly	Weekly
Phone calls and e-mail	As needed	As needed	As needed	As needed
Team meetings	Minutes weekly	As needed	Attends weekly	Attends weekly
Status report on project web site	Daily	Daily	Daily	Daily

Figure 25-2. Communication process.

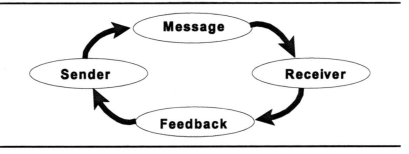

attitudes, beliefs, perceptions, education, language, culture, and emotions. Communication is successful if the decoded message is the same as the sender intended.

BARRIERS TO COMMUNICATION

The chart in Figure 25-3 shows common barriers to communication with examples of each. These barriers may disrupt communication or stop it all together.

Communication may also be complicated by the number of people involved. Each additional individual involved in communication significantly increases the number of interactions and communications requirements (see Figure 25-4). It is difficult for a project manager to communicate on a regular basis with more than six to eight key people.

IMPROVING YOUR COMMUNICATION SKILLS

You can improve communication by taking the following actions:

- Choose the most appropriate method of transmission for your communication: face-to-face, telephone conversation, voice mail, e-mail, video conference, memo, letter, etc. Determine which method is most appropriate considering the urgency

Figure 25-3. Common barriers to communication.

Category	Examples
Logistics	■ Geography ■ Time zones ■ Method (face-to-face, telephone, voice mail, memo, e-mail) ■ Culture (from country to country or even within the same country)
Language	■ Terminology (jargon) ■ Nonverbal (gestures, tone, body language) ■ Mother tongue vs. learned language ■ Mistranslations
People	■ Background (frame of reference) ■ Education ■ Values ■ Attitudes ■ Social status
Organization	■ Organizational culture ■ Rumor (grapevine) ■ Conflicting priorities ■ Departmental relationships ■ Territorial issues

and importance of the message or the need to discuss the issue, make a decision, or negotiate.

■ Prepare your message in advance. Determine how and when to deliver the message. Identify the problem that needs action, gather relevant information, and focus on the most important issues.

■ Deliver the message in a clear and constructive way. Use appropriate nonverbal communication. Be aware of the other person's feelings and show genuine concern.

■ Listen to the receiver's message. Really listen. Ask questions until you are sure you understand the response. Accept the fact that the other person may see things differently from how you see them.

■ Verify understanding by summarizing or paraphrasing the response to be sure you understand correctly.

Figure 25-4. Number of people involved in communications.

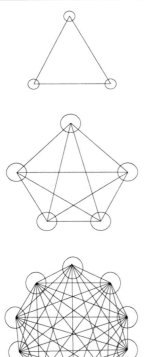

3 individuals
3 potential interactions

5 individuals
10 potential interactions

10 individuals
45 potential interactions

$$interactions = \frac{individuals \times (individuals - 1)}{2}$$

Listening

Listening is a critical part of communication. The purpose of listening is to understand the message from the point of view of the other person rather than filter it through your own frame of reference. Effective project managers take the time and effort to carefully listen to others.

Listening is not discussion. Listening is a one-way process that involves hearing and understanding the message the another person is conveying. Discussing, on the other hand, is a two-way interchange of ideas. Effective listening requires full attention, rather than the rapid switching between listening and talking that is involved in discussion. This rapid switching can prevent the more intensive, careful listening that allows the speakers to reveal their feelings.

Listening is not problem solving. Listen to understand—not to propose solutions. Finding solutions might be a next step, but it is not part of the listening process. In fact, moving too quickly from listening to proposing solutions may interfere with the communication process. If you impose your solution without giving others a chance to be heard, they may stop coming to you with problems and questions.

The purpose of listening is to understand the message from the point of view of the other person. Understanding the other person does not mean you agree with him. Whether you agree is not the issue in the listening process.

The following actions can help you improve your listening skills:

- Listen intently, concentrating on the individual and what is being said. Listen for content, not just verbiage. Listen to the emotions and needs being expressed. Read between the lines and try to understand the other person's point of view.

- Seek clarification and confirmation. If a person makes a request or provides information, clarify what was said so that you both are sure the message has been conveyed correctly.

- Resist the urge to correct errors made by the speaker. When people express strong feelings, they often exaggerate or overstate the facts—sometimes in anger and with accusations. As you listen, concentrate on hearing the message rather than correcting the facts.

■   Don't allow biases to interfere. People tend to pay more attention to some people than to others, and to give certain information more credence because of who delivers it. If you assume that the information is important, regardless of who delivers it, you are more likely to remember it.

Nonverbal Communication

We communicate in many more ways than just talking. We also communicate nonverbally by our body language, such as eye contact, expressions, gestures, body movements, and body positioning.

Nonverbal communication affects both the speaker and listener. Negative nonverbal feedback can cause the speaker to lose concentration, drift off the topic, and get discouraged. In such communications, the listener cannot organize his thoughts or recall important information.

Focused Conversation

Workers who are not performing may try to steer you away from the conversation at hand. You can direct a conversation and keep the speaker on track without being rude or discourteous if you follow four basic steps:

1. *State the purpose of the conversation (or ask the other person to state her purpose.* This step can be brief, but helps establish a common understanding of the purpose of the conversation. For example, "Let's talk for a few minutes about the problems we're having

getting on-time delivery of raw materials. We talked yesterday about the vendor's transportation problems, so let's focus today on problems we may be having in placing orders." Such a brief sentence or two can help get the conversation focused quickly and reduce the chance of misunderstandings and conflict.

2. *Gather information using open- and closed-ended questions.* Closed-ended questions are usually answered with "yes," "no," or a specific piece of information. For example, "Did you receive the materials on time?" or "What was the cost of that activity?" Open-ended questions require more thought and usually provide more insight. For example, "Why do you think we are having problems with on-time delivery of materials?" or "What can we do to decrease the cost of that activity?"

3. *Verify understanding by paraphrasing or summarizing (or ask the other person to summarize).* This step involves more than merely parroting back information. The focus should be on summarizing key points or assignments to be sure that there is clear understanding.

4. *Direct the conversation by using questions and nonverbal behavior.* When there is a problem or conflict, the other person may try to steer the conversation away from the points you want to discuss. Keep the conversation focused on the issues at hand by using tactful questions and body language.

DEFINITIONS

Communication plan. A description of what information is communicated, to whom, how, and how often.

APPLICATION EXERCISES

1. To understand how nonverbal behavior can influence communication, try the following exercise with a friend: In thirty seconds or less, tell your friend about your current project. Show enthu-

siasm and try to get your friend interested in the project. Your friend's job is to use body language and nonverbal behavior that shows total disinterest. You may be surprised how much nonverbal behavior affects both the speaker and listener.

2. Consider how you will offer feedback to a project team member. Considering the suggestions in this chapter, write down specific plans.

3. Practice using the four basic steps of focused conversation. Ask your friend to play the part of a project team member who is behind schedule on a project task. Instruct your friend to be defensive and not offer detailed information unless specifically asked. You play the part of the project manager who is determined to get to the bottom of the project delay.

APPLICATION QUESTIONS

1. Are you satisfied with how effectively you communicate?

2. Are you satisfied with how effectively your team communicates? What can you do to improve your listening skills?

CASE STUDY ❖❖❖❖❖❖❖❖❖

Global Industries

Global Industries prepares an annual stockholder report in ten languages. This year's report gives important information about a pending merger that requires a vote at the annual stockholders meeting on June 3. Therefore, the president requested that the ten versions of the report be mailed by May 1. On March 1, Larry, the project manager, scheduled the four-week's work of editing and designing the primary document (in English) to be completed by

April 1. This would give time for translation, graphic production, and printing in the other nine languages by May 1.

The project team consists of an editor and a designer located at company headquarters, nine language translators located in various countries, and customer services representatives from five printing companies also located in various countries. At the beginning of the project, Larry set up a telephone conference call with all members of the team to explain the project objectives and schedules. Because the representatives from the printing companies didn't speak English very well, Larry was careful to speak slowly and clearly. He asked each team member to provide a status report every two weeks.

In the beginning, Larry was confident that the schedules would be met, but at the first status report, the editor informed him that she was ten days behind in writing the report because the president had not returned her phone calls requesting clarification on some details of the merger. Furthermore, the designer and editor couldn't agree on the basic design of the report. The editor wanted a formal, traditional design and the designer wanted an informal, modern layout.

What potential problems do you see in Larry's communication plan? What communication barriers exist and how would you solve them? What conflicts exist and how would you resolve them?

(Suggested answers are given in Appendix A at the back of the book.)

❖❖❖

CHAPTER

26

HOLDING EFFECTIVE MEETINGS

Running an effective meeting requires planning and effort. When a project manager needs to find out or disseminate information, she may be tempted to call a meeting. Although this may be a quick solution for her, it may not be the best use of everyone's time. She may need to use other methods so team members can stay focused on the work at hand.

Meetings are essential for building teams, solving group problems, making group decisions, and achieving group consensus.

This chapter suggests ways to make meetings more effective, including the use of an agenda and other tools.

PREPARING FOR MEETINGS

You must plan and prepare for a meeting to make it an efficient use of time for all who attend.

Purpose and Format of the Meeting

A meeting is most effective as a forum for discussion, brainstorming, problem-solving, decision-making, coordinating, and improving communication and relationships between individuals or departments. Fact-finding and disseminating information can often be handled more effectively in other ways.

Consider the appropriate format (directed discussion, open discussion) to achieve the desired result.

Scheduling Meetings

Avoid holding meetings at the busiest times. When people have other things on their minds, they will not be productive participants. Set time limits for meetings and don't worry if they run shorter. Be creative by calling a meeting to begin at 8:13 A.M. or set a 23-minute time limit for the meeting. Schedule hour meetings to last no longer than 50 minutes to give participants time to get to their next appointments.

Determining Whom to Invite

Carefully consider the list of people to invite to a meeting. If the meeting is too large, it may be impossible to accomplish the business at hand. On the other hand, if too few are invited, the attendees may lack the information, experience, or knowledge needed to deal with the issues. Also consider the positions (levels) of the people involved. Do you need a meeting of people who are empowered to make a decision or do you need the workers who have first-hand knowledge of the situation?

Agenda

A simple agenda—even a handwritten list—may be sufficient for an informal meeting where team members discuss a handful of uncomplicated items. But as meetings grow in size, involve more individuals at different levels in the organization, and focus on more complex issues, an agenda needs to be more formal and exact.

Meetings can be more effective when an agenda is prepared and distributed before the meeting. This advanced notice gives presenters the information they need to appropriately prepare their presentations and attendees can review the topics and come prepared for discussions. Attach any materials the attendees should review before the meeting. The sample agenda in Figure 26-1 shows a helpful format. Adapt it to the particular needs of your organization.

Figure 26–1. Sample agenda.

Agenda

Date: 5 December 2004
Where: East Boardroom

Attending: Larry Smith, Scott Johnson, Brent Andersen, Ron Biltmore.

Objective: Plan the publication of the annual stockholders report.

What	Who	How long	Notes
1. Review proposed publication: ■ why needed ■ who will use it ■ discuss specifications	Larry	5 min	
2. Concerns about its use and need	Scott	5 min	
3. Discuss production steps: ■ who ■ resources needed ■ time frames ■ impact on other jobs in process	Brent	10 min	
4. Create tentative schedule.	Larry	3 min	
5. Give go-ahead to designer and editor.	Ron	1 min	

After preparing the agenda, ask yourself again whether there is a real need for the meeting. See whether you can turn the agenda into a memo and skip holding the meeting.

CONDUCTING MEETINGS

At the beginning of the meeting, state the purpose of the meeting to confirm the understanding with everyone in attendance. If all agenda items don't pertain to everyone at the meeting, try to cover the general topics first and dismiss people as appropriate.

The responsibility of the person conducting the meeting is to achieve the purpose of the meeting and make it an efficient use of everyone's time. Therefore, keep discussions focused on the agenda and deviate from it only when it makes sense to do so.

The following techniques may be helpful to keep the meeting focused.

Group Memory

Using the group memory tool, the meeting leader writes brief lists on large sheets of paper or a whiteboard (see Figure 26-2). The purpose is to capture ideas, discussions, and decisions.

- Use key words. Abbreviate.
- Use speaker's own words.
- Print large and use colors.
- Keep sheets in view.

The benefits of group memory are the following:

Figure 26-2. Group memory tool.

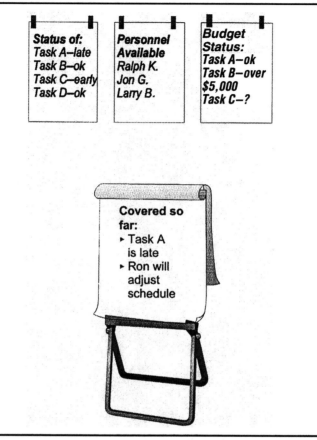

- It keeps group on task.
- It provides quick recall.
- It prevents backtracking.
- It reduces trivial pursuits.

Issues List

An issues list (see Figure 26-3) can be used to keep a meeting focused. It is used to list issues or ideas that come up in conversation but that are not the main topic of the discussion. Writing the issues on a list shows the meeting participants that you care

Figure 26-3. Sample issues list.

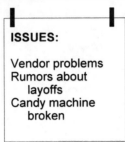

about their issues and have noted them for later discussion, but be sure that you hold follow-up discussions to cover the issues on the list.

Next Steps

A list of next steps (see Figure 26-4) can also be kept to record ideas as they come up. By recording them on a list you force commitment.

APPLICATION QUESTIONS

1. How well do you run meetings? What techniques from this chapter do you want to implement to improve your meetings?
2. For your current project, describe when it would be appropriate to hold a meeting and when other methods of communication should be used.

Figure 26-4. Sample next steps list.

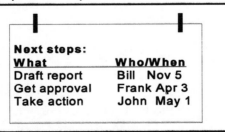

MAKING TEAM DECISIONS

During the course of a project, many decisions are made each day that ultimately affect the project for good or ill. Some are small decisions with relatively little impact, whereas others have major impact.

Some decisions are made by the project man-
ager with little or no input from the team. Other decisions are more important and require that the project manager get more information from the team or the support of the team. In such cases, the project manager may wish to make a group decision with the project team.

The guidelines in this chapter can help the project manager determine when and how to involve others in a decision. Involving other people in a decision offers both advantages and disadvantages. Advantages of a group decision are as follows:

- ■ It provides a broader perspective.
- ■ It contributes more experience and ideas.
- ■ It gets the commitment of others in the decision.

The disadvantages of involving others in a decision include the following:

- You must be willing to negotiate.
- The meeting may be more difficult to control—it may get bogged down because of the size of the group.
- The decision may alienate some people—you can't please everyone.
- Not everyone has helpful insights or expertise.

When to Involve Others

In most cases, it will be obvious when you need to involve others. When it is less readily apparent, a good rule of thumb is to include others when:

- You need their commitment.
- You don't have the expertise.

When Not to Involve Others

It is usually not a good idea to involve others in a decision in the following conditions:

- The decision is about a trivial issue.
- The decision involves a personnel issue.
- You are unable or unwilling to negotiate.
- You need a quick decision and you have adequate expertise (when the need for speed is greater than the need for commitment).

Whom to Involve

All too often, we surround ourselves with people who think and act like we do. But remember that two heads are better than one only if they disagree. The following adaptation of a popular saying gives good advice for providing the needed diversity:

Someone old: One who has been around a long time

Someone new: One who has new ideas

Someone borrowed: A person from a user or requestor group or from another department in the organization

Someone blue: A devil's advocate who asks the tough questions

Team Decision Making

When you determine to make a decision as a team, be prepared to take the time needed and be willing to respect the decision of the group. Consider the following guidelines:

- ■ The leader sets the agenda.
- ■ All team members take an active role.
- ■ Each person listens with respect.
- ■ Each person expresses his or her point of view.
- ■ The team focuses on what is best for the organization.
- ■ The decision is made by the group, and the group agrees on appropriate assignments, follow-up, and evaluation.

Following these guidelines can help the project manager make better decisions that involve the project team when appropriate.

APPLICATION QUESTIONS

1. How well do you make decisions individually? How could a team decision-making process lead to a better decision?

2. Considering your current project, what problems are appropriate for team decisions?

28

USING SOURCES OF POWER WISELY

People regularly associate power with authority, and most people believe that if they just had more authority they could accomplish what they want to do.

This chapter discusses the need for power, the types and sources of power, and how to negotiate for the power you need.

THE NEED FOR POWER

Project managers may not always have direct authority over the team members they must rely on to get things done. Furthermore, traditional authoritarian methods don't work in the new team environment, where the roles of superior ("boss") and subordinate ("worker") have given way to more equal adult-to-adult relationships.

To get things done, project managers must create and nurture useful bases of power.

SOURCES OF POWER

Power comes from one of the basic sources listed below. Project managers need two or three of these sources to be successful.

Expert

Expert power is the ability to gain support because people perceive that the project manager has special knowledge or expertise they consider important. Even if the manager doesn't actually have the knowledge or expertise, he may possess expert power if others perceive he does.

Relationship

Relationship power is the ability to gain support because others feel they have a caring work relationship with the project manager. Team members feel close to the manager and desire to support her because of the friendship they have developed. Since they feel she cares about them, they are willing to follow her lead.

Referent

Referent power is the ability to gain support because of the desire of others to identify with the project manager or the project. Team members may support the project manager because he is seen as a leader and they want to gain from the implied credibility they will receive by associating with him. Likewise, team members may want to be involved in a successful, high-profile project to give them visibility or status in the organization.

Expert, relationship, and referent power are sources of personal power that come from personal characteristics. They emanate from an individual's personality and attitudes rather than from his position or title. These three sources of power are effective, and the more they are used the more the base of power grows.

Authority

Authority power is the ability to gain support because others perceive the project manager has the power to issue orders. This source of power is called "position power" because it comes from the position a person holds.

Reward

Reward power is the ability to gain support because people perceive that the project manager is capable of directly or indirectly dispensing valued rewards, such as salary increases, bonuses, promotions, better office space, furniture, equipment, future work assignments, or fund allocations.

Penalty

Penalty power is the ability to gain support because others perceive that the project manager is capable of directly or indirectly dispensing penalties or negative consequences. Penalty power usually derives from the same sources as reward power, with one being a necessary condition for the other.

Authority, reward, and penalty are all referred to as "position power." This power is not earned, but delegated to the manager because of her title or position. Although this power has its legitimate uses, it should not be over-used. It is not the most effective ways to inspire and motivate.

TYPES OF POWER

The three main types of power are influence, negotiation, and coercion.

Influence

Influence is sharing power and getting others to cooperate for common goals. It is the most practical strategy to use. It is low cost, good politics, and effective no matter what your formal level of authority.

Negotiation

Negotiation is trading for power. This win-win strategy is good for both parties because neither feels taken advantage of. Negotiation is often used between people of differing levels of authority where influence alone is not effective. It is also a useful strategy when you feel that there is a high risk that you will not get what you need.

Coercion

Coercion is imposing power through formal organizational lines. It is generally the least practical and, politically, the most expensive strategy to use. It should be used only as a last resort.

Some project managers start out trying to accomplish a project goal by influencing others, then get confused between the project's needs and their own emotional needs for control, and finally revert to coercion. Team members may get confused over the same issues. When this happens, we often refer to it as "politics" or a "power struggle."

WINNING STRATEGIES FOR NEGOTIATING AND SHARING POWER

People have emotional needs to be in control or to avoid being controlled. We all want to be recognized and respected by other people, and these emotional needs are easily stirred when one person tries to get another to do something. We constantly share power with others in the team environment.

Trust and good will are key to building relationships where power is shared. Such relationships are facilitated in an environment where people focus on facts and work content rather than emotions.

The first step in determining how to negotiate or share power is to clearly understand what you want and need as well as what the other person wants and needs. Determine what you are willing and not willing to give up to get what you want and then try to determine what the other party might be willing to give up. Using a chart like the one shown in Figure 28-1 may help you determine what can be negotiated so that both parties' wants and needs can be met.

Suppose the project manager needs to confront a team member who is not performing. Before launching into the interaction, the project manager may want to take a moment to determine the best strategy, so that the interaction will build (and not damage) the relationship. In such cases it is usually helpful to focus on long-term goals rather than short-term gains.

When you negotiate or share power with another person, keep in mind the following key steps:

- Make clear the goal of the organization and the project and establish that "we are all in this together."
- State what *you* need to be successful. (Tap their power sources.)

Figure 28-1. Negotiating power: determining needs and wants.

My needs	Other party's ability to provide
Needs: Wants:	
Other party's needs	*My ability to provide*
Needs: Wants:	

- Ask what *they* need from you to be successful. (Offer to share your power.)
- Resolve the difference between your position and the other party's position.
- Reach agreement.

APPLICATION QUESTIONS

1. What sources of power described in this chapter are available to you? How can you most effectively use each one?

2. How will you implement ideas from this chapter to negotiate or share power more effectively?

❖ ❖ ❖

CHAPTER 29

MANAGING CHANGE

Because change is a product or byproduct of most projects, you must deal with the fears and perceptions of the people involved and manage the process of change. People do not welcome a new and better way simply because it is new and better. People resist change because it upsets their familiar environment and makes them feel insecure.

The process of change may require people to let go of the past and accept new processes or environments. This change may be disruptive, slow, and difficult to manage. Thus, you need to consider what changes will be required of people and determine how you will manage the process of change. Before you jump into managing the change, consider the issues in this chapter that may have a major impact on your success in managing change.

GUIDELINES FOR MANAGING CHANGE

Identify the Problem

Clearly identify the reasons for the change and the impact the changes will have on the people involved. Although they may be obvious to you as the project manager, other people who will be affected may not have the same vision. Determine exactly what needs to change, and when, how fast, and how much. Describe the payoffs and the risks involved.

Create a Transition Plan

In creating a transition plan, involve the people who will be effected by the change. Give them a chance to study the old methods and the proposed changes and suggest other possibilities. Help them gain a positive attitude about the change and ask for their cooperation.

Create a team to manage the transition. Have a plan in place to anticipate problems and coordinate the change process.

Sell people on the *personal benefits* of the change rather than the *features* of the product or service. They won't care that it works better unless they can clearly see how it will benefit them. The following are potential personal benefits. Consider which of these benefits apply to your current project and how you would provide them.

- Adventure
- Affection
- Appearance
- Comfort
- Convenience
- Dependability
- Ease of operation

- Economy
- Efficiency
- Fear
- Health
- Play and recreation
- Prestige
- Pride
- Protection
- Recognition
- Service

Implement the Plan

Carefully articulate the reasons for the change and its potential impact on the people involved. Explain why, when, how fast, and how much. Describe to everyone affected by the change the payoffs and the risks. Explain what would happen if the change were not implemented.

Communicate regularly with people, both individually and in groups. Keep them aware of the progress and listen to their concerns. Acknowledge and reward efforts. As change begins to take place, recognize the achievements of the people who made it happen. Acknowledge their struggles and sacrifices.

APPLICATION EXERCISE

1. Identify a change that will be a result of your current project. Define the change carefully in terms of who will be effected and how.

2. Create a transition plan, including who would be involved and what the expected outcome would be. Explain how the plan would be implemented.

CHAPTER 30

MANAGING PERFORMANCE

A primary job of the project manager is to manage project performance. This chapter describes a performance management system and gives ideas on how to develop a performance management plan. It also provides suggestions on how to use feedback effectively.

PERFORMANCE MANAGEMENT

Performance management is the on-going process of minimizing the number and impact of problems and providing an environment wherein the project can succeed.

Figure 30-1 illustrates a performance management system. A request for action should always be followed by feedback and consequences. When you ask a team member to perform a task, you need to provide positive feedback if it was done well and constructive criticism if her performance needs to improve. You also need to provide positive or negative consequences. In the

Figure 30-1. Performance management system.

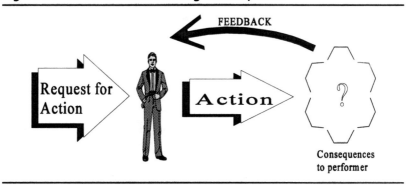

absence of feedback and consequences, the quality of performance will decline or the performance will stop all together.

Take the following steps to manage performance:

- Establish a clear goal.

- Request action.

- Give feedback. Determine beforehand what feedback is needed to keep performance on track, when, and how often.

- Administer consequences. Determine beforehand the consequence to workers for performance or nonperformance.

- Manage the environment by removing obstacles and providing resources and other conditions for success.

MANAGING BY MEASUREMENT

Managers often manage by observing workers, which is also called "management by walking around." Although it can provide valuable first-hand information, it has the following disadvantages:

- It is frequently out of context and may be inaccurate.

- It sees activities rather than results.

- It often focuses on the negative. The employee seldom wins.

A more effective method for project managers is management by measurement. This involves measuring performance based on project objectives and has the following advantages:

- It is more accurate and is self-correcting over time.

- It focuses on results and keeps the focus on critical information.

- It focuses on the positive. The employee can win.

When performance is measured, performance improves. When performance is measured and reported, the rate of improvement accelerates.

Have the courage to keep score; don't keep track of excuses. (Many people would rather not know the score than run the risk of knowing they are losing!)

PERFORMANCE MANAGEMENT PLAN

Use the following four steps to develop a performance management plan:

1. Write a clear goal statement describing the deliverable you need. Describe what you need and when you need it.

2. Describe the feedback you will use to keep performance on track. Determine the methods will you use to give feedback. Describe the timing of the feedback in terms of frequency or dates.

3. Plan the consequences. Describe what will happen to the performer as a result of performing or not performing. If there is no natural consequence, you must create one using feedback.

4. Determine the factors in the performer's environment that could interfere with the performance and find a way to reduce the likelihood or impact of those factors.

USING FEEDBACK EFFECTIVELY

Feedback is a way of making people aware of how their behavior affects others. Just as a guided missile system continuously corrects the course of a missile, feedback helps individuals keep their behavior "on target" and thus better achieve their goals. Consider the following suggestions as you plan the feedback you will give.

- ■ Make feedback descriptive rather than evaluative. Describe the behavior you see and its effect on you without evaluating or imagining the reason for the behavior. This reduces the need for the individual to respond defensively. An evaluative example: "You were deliberately tapping your foot to distract me." A descriptive example: "When I was talking you were tapping your foot, and I found it hard to concentrate on what I was saying."

- ■ Make feedback specific rather than general. A general example would be: "You're careless." A specific example would be: "Yesterday's report had several grammatical errors and the chart on page 4 presented the wrong information."

- ■ Direct the feedback toward a behavior the person can do something about. It only increases frustration when a person is reminded of a shortcoming over which she has no control. Not helpful: "Sally, you shouldn't be so shy." More helpful: "Sally, I'd like you to present the budget figures in tomorrow's project meeting. I'd be happy to review them with you before the meeting and give you some ideas on what to say about them."

■ Give feedback immediately. Feedback given on the spot is more meaningful because the situation surrounding the behavior is fresh in the person's mind. A poorly-timed example: "Hey Bob, that class you gave last month was great." A well-timed example: "Bob, I really liked that class you just gave. I found it to be interesting and to the point, and you were easy to understand."

■ Limit feedback to a few items. Giving too much feedback may cause the person to become defensive.

■ Encourage an environment where feedback is welcomed. If feedback is threatening, people will dread giving and receiving it. The ideal situation is to give feedback only when requested. Such feedback is more useful and is usually better accepted than unsolicited feedback. Because some people may never request feedback, if you feel it is important you might say "John, you haven't asked for it, but I have some feedback for you if you want it." This lets John know you care and gives him the option to ask for the feedback.

■ Use feedback to help the person become more effective. If your intent is to punish or get even, your feedback will not be effective. Feedback is a corrective mechanism for an individual who wants to learn to match behavior to his or her intentions.

DEFINITIONS

Performance management. The on-going process of minimizing the number and impact of problems and providing an environment wherein the project can succeed.

APPLICATION EXERCISE

Think of a project activity that needs to be accomplished by someone else. Choose someone who has a nonsubordinate relationship to you (that is, you do not pay them, nor do you conduct or contribute to their performance review). Review the four steps listed above to develop a performance plan for your project activity.

APPLICATION QUESTIONS

1. In your current project, what can you do to improve how you manage performance?

2. What feedback and consequences can you provide to people working on your current project?

3. Why is management by measurement effective for project managers?

4. What measurements are needed to effectively manage your current project?

CASE STUDY ❖❖❖❖❖❖❖❖❖

Chip Technologies

In response to increasing competition by computer chip manufacturers, Chip Technologies held a series of strategy meetings to determine their future direction. Dan, one of the vice presidents, proposed a new product he felt could become a major product for the company. The president liked Dan's idea and appointed Jan as project manager of a team to develop a comprehensive plan for its development, manufacture, and marketing. Jan was an aggressive new employee who had the confidence of the president. Although Dan was not an official member of the project team, he wanted to maintain a high profile in the project and be recognized as a major reason for its success.

Dan began attending project meetings and asked to review all recommendations before they were presented to upper management. He told Jan that he was to approve all project expenses and use of company resources. Jan consented to his requests because he was a vice president and had initiated the idea for the product.

Jan requested that five engineers be assigned to the project. Bob, the functional manager over engineering, provided only three engineers because he was skeptical of the product idea and he had designs of his own he wanted to develop. Bob had been with the company for twenty years and resented the fact that an employee as new as Jan was given such an important project.

In frustration, Jan became more aggressive and insisted that Bob provide all five engineers. When he refused, she made vigorous attempts to gain control of the issue, including belittling him in front of other employees. In a project meeting, when Dan announced he would not approve an important project expense, Jan openly challenged his authority and threatened to take it to the company president.

Identify the power struggles in this case study and propose solutions.

(Suggested answers are given in Appendix A at the back of the book.)

ANSWERS TO EXERCISES AND CASE STUDIES

CHAPTER 5

Case Study: CXI Cellular

This case study illustrates mistakes commonly made in managing projects. Some of these problems are listed below, along with suggestions on what Robert (the project manager) could do to help the project succeed.

Understanding of Project Management Principles

The company appears not to know much about project management. For example, the vice president of marketing appointed Robert to be the project manager. Why is marketing taking the lead in managing an engineering and manufacturing project?

Robert was also asked to develop a schedule and budget in a week for a large project. Robert may need to take steps to educate the management team about project management if, indeed, he knows much about project management himself, given that his background is in sales.

Definition of Roles and Responsibilities

The vice president of marketing appointed Robert to be the project manager. Later, the COO asks Robert to report directly to him. Robert needs to clarify his role as a project manager and clearly define the reporting relationships. He needs to define his authority to form and manage a project team. He also needs to be given financial authority to approve project expenses himself, at least up to a certain dollar amount.

Skills of the Project Manager

Robert was the top salesman in the marketing department, yet he was chosen to be the project manager. Being a good salesman does not qualify him to be a good project manager. If he doesn't somehow acquire project management skills quickly, the project will fail. Not only will the company lose financially with a failed project, but they will also lose out on the sales Robert would have made if he had been left in marketing.

Approval and Buy-In by Management

When Robert presented his plans to the executive management team, there was considerable discussion about whether the company should begin manufacturing the new phone. Robert needs the approval and support of the management team. While the COO's support is helpful, it will not be sufficient to accomplish such a large engineering and manufacturing project.

CHAPTER 9

Application Exercise: Picnic at the Lake

The chart in Figure A-1 shows the preceding activities. Figure A-2 shows the network diagram based on the information in Figure A-1.

Case Study: Geebold Manufacturing

This case study illustrates mistakes commonly made by project managers in planning projects. In her enthusiasm, Ann has spent five months planning and estimating the project all by herself. Although she may be complimented on her diligence, she appears to lack common sense. She should have used those five months involving the project team from the beginning of the planning process. The team members should have helped to develop the work breakdown structure, provided the estimates, and given input on all phases of planning. Not only may Ann's plans have serious faults, it may now be difficult for Ann to get

Figure A-1. Picnic at the lake: preceding activities.

Activity Description	Person Responsible	Duration (mins.)	Preceding activity
1. Decide on trip	Husband & wife	2	none
2. Get money from bank	Husband	12	1
3. Boil eggs	Wife	10	1
4. Make egg sandwiches	Wife	10	3
5. Load car	Husband & wife	5	2, 4
6. Drive to lake	Husband & wife	30	5

Figure A-2. Picnic at the lake: network diagram.

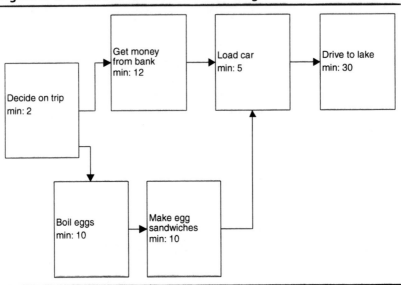

the support of the project team when she presents the plans to them.

Project Objectives

It appears that she carefully defined the project objectives of cost, time, and scope, and she wisely got the approval of the board of directors on the scope statement.

Project Reviews

No mention is made of project reviews, such as a conceptual review, feasibility study, benefit-cost analysis, alternative course of action review, or risk assessment. These are critical in a large project.

Work Breakdown Structure

The work breakdown structure appears to be imbalanced. Typically, the work packages should represent eight to eighty hours of work. Her packages with two to three hours of work are probably too detailed to be scheduled and managed by the project manager. The packages with 150 hours of work probably need to be broken down further.

Estimating

Ann estimated each of the activities using an analogous approach, drawing on plans she discovered of a similar project that the company had planned three years ago but never completed. The time and costs in these three-year-old plans need to be verified in the current economy. Further, because this old plan was never executed, the assumptions in the plan should be carefully tested. She should have used skilled team members to create accurate plans and estimates. Parametric estimating may be more appropriate for this construction project, or even a bottom-up estimate because she has created a very detailed work breakdown structure.

Sequencing the Activities

Ann has drawn a network diagram showing the sequence each activity and their interrelationships. As she involves the project team in the planning process, she should verify the accuracy of the diagram with the team.

CHAPTER 15

Case Study: Urgent Care Hospital

This case study asks you to find a way to crash the schedule. Although the four activities could be done in sequence (one after another), the schedule can be fast tracked by beginning the training before the renovation is completed. As a result, two activities can be performed in parallel (at the same time) and the project can be completed two weeks sooner, as illustrated in Figure A-3.

Figure A-4 is the network diagram based on the information in the chart in Figure A-3. The scheduled dates have been included.

The cash flow report in Figure A-5 shows the projected expenditures during each week of the project.

CHAPTER 17

Application Exercise #5: Earned Value Calculations

The following explains the calculations of the schedule and cost variances and the schedule and cost indices in the exercise.

The planned value (PV) is the planned cost of work scheduled to be done in a given time period. In this example, it is $1,500, because all work was scheduled to be completed by today.

The earned value (EV) is the planned cost of work actually performed. Since only two-thirds of the planned work has actually been performed as of today, the EV is 2/3 of $1,500, or $1,000.

Figure A–3. CATSCAN project: crashed schedule.

Activity Description	Duration (weeks)	Preceding activity
1. Receive CATSCAN	0	None
2. Install CATSCAN	3	1
3. Renovate radiology department	8	2
4. Train CATSCAN operators	2	2
5. End	0	3, 4

Figure A–4. CATSCAN project: network diagram.

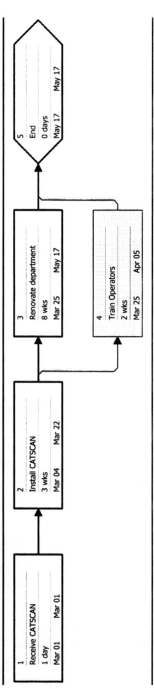

Figure A-5. CATSCAN project: anticipated cash flow.

Cost categories	Weeks												Total (in 000s)
	0	1	2	3	4	5	6	7	8	9	10	11	
Purchase	$1,000												$1,000
Installation		$15	$15	$15									$45
Renovation					$12	$12	$12	$12	$12	$12	$12	$12	$96
Training											$8	$8	$16
Total	$1,000	$15	$15	$15	$12	$12	$12	$12	$12	$12	$20	$20	$1,157

The actual cost (AC) is the cost incurred to complete the work actually performed as of today. The exercise stated the amount as $1,350.

The schedule variance is earned value minus planned value, or SV = EV − PV. In this example, $1,000 − $1,500 = − $500. This calculation measures the difference between the planned and the actual work completed. The large negative result means the project is significantly behind schedule.

The cost variance is earned value minus actual cost, or CV = EV − AC. In this example, $1,000 − $1,350 = − $350. This calculation measures the difference between the planned (budgeted) cost and the actual cost of work completed. The negative result means the project is over budget.

The schedule performance index is earned value divided by planned value, or SPI = EV / PV. In this example, $1,000 / $1,500 = .67. This ratio is a measure of efficiency in the schedule. Since the value is significantly less than1, it indicates that the project has accomplished less than planned and is significantly behind schedule.

The cost performance index is earned value divided by actual cost, or CPI = EV / AC. In this example, $1,000 / $1,350 = .74. This ratio is a measure of cost efficiency (how efficiently dollars are being spent). Since the value is less than 1, it indicates that the project is costing more than planned. Each $1.00 spent on the project has produced only $0.74 worth of value.

CHAPTER 22

Case Study: Western Power

The major areas of concern in the case study are listed below. Many of the control processes discussed in Section 3 could be implemented to better control this project.

Project Objectives

The project objectives of time, cost, and scope must be carefully managed in this project. In the beginning, management was anxious to complete the project as soon as possible because of the plant's anticipated revenue. Time was of the essence, especially when lawsuits delayed the start of construction by a few months. However, shortly after construction began it was determined that the plant would not produce the expected revenue, and management's focus shifted to controlling and reducing costs. One year into the project, it was discovered that scope and quality were not being adequately controlled and the resulting rework had additional impact on both budget and schedule.

As the new project manager, you should discuss various recovery options with company executives. With deficits in all three areas (time, cost, and scope), you need clear direction from them on priorities, since recovery in any one of the three areas will likely impact the other two.

Project Change Control

It appears there was little or no formal process to control changes made in design and construction. This is a major error in a project of this magnitude. As the new project manager, you should implement a formal process to submit, evaluate, approve, and communicate changes in the project plan. Your process should focus on improving communication and agreement between all parties involved (engineers, architects, construction managers, and workers).

Project Risk

The numerous design changes may also be an indication of the risk of implementing new technologies in this innovative power plant. The architects and engineers often couldn't agree on how the plant should best be constructed to make the new technologies work. As the new project manager, you should carefully analyze the risks and develop both preventive and contingency plans. Be sure the company management understands the risks involved.

Quality Control

The fact that portions of the construction do not meet government standards and must be rebuilt is an indication that quality is not being controlled. In addition to the cost and time required for rework, news reports of poor quality may cause further public relations problems. As the new project manager, you need to ensure that quality standards are clearly communicated and monitored. This project undoubtedly requires a formal quality assurance team to audit work against the quality standards and ensure that workers have the proper skills to do quality work.

Time Control

The project started a few months late because of pending lawsuits. The numerous design changes and rework added another few months delay. As the new project manager, you should carefully review existing time control procedures. Be sure that schedule data is being collected, evaluated, and reported in appropriate ways. Implement routine project evaluations, which could have uncovered problem areas sooner.

As mentioned previously, you should discuss various recovery options with company executives. With deficits in time, cost, and scope, you need clear direction from them on priorities, since recovery from the six-month delay in project schedule will likely impact both cost and project scope. If it is determined to make up some or all of the time, various strategies may be employed to crash the schedule, such as finding a different approach to complete the project, modifying the project objectives, increasing personnel, scheduling shift work, or running some activities in parallel.

Cost Control

The numerous design changes and rework may be contributing to the cost overruns. As the new project manager, carefully review existing cost control procedures. Ensure that financial data is being collected, evaluated, and reported in appropriate ways to control costs. It is likely that routine project evaluations could have uncovered problem areas sooner.

As mentioned previously, you should discuss various recovery options with company executives. With deficits in time, cost, and scope, you need clear direction from them on priorities, since recovery from the ten percent cost overrun will likely impact both schedule and project scope. If it is determined to make up some or all of the cost overrun, it will likely be necessary to reduce the project scope and find less costly ways to complete the rest of the project.

Financial Justification for the Project

It appears that Western Power did not do their homework before launching the project. Since the company didn't begin negotiating contracts with other utility companies until after construction began, they discovered too late that their return on investment would not be what they anticipated. They then asked the project manager to reduce the construction budget to maintain the expected level of profitability. This was a difficult request for a tightly-regulated, high-profile construction project. Unfortunately, the project manager's efforts to reduce costs produced confusion, rework, higher costs, and greater delays.

CHAPTER 25

Case Study: Global Industries

This case presents typical issues in communications and conflict resolution.

Communication Plan

Larry began well by gathering the entire team together in a conference call to explain the project objectives and schedules. Because the team was dispersed in several countries, this conference call was probably the next best option to having a face-to-face meeting. However, because several team members are not native English speakers, Larry needs to be sure they understand his communications with them. He could consider using the translators to interpret his communications into the languages spoken by the representatives from the printing companies.

A fault in the communication plan appears to be the frequency of status reports. Since the major project tasks are in increments of one month, a status report every two weeks is not often enough to spot potential problems in time to take corrective action before the problems become serious. For example, at the end of the first two-week period, the project manager discovered the project was already ten days late. Status reporting on this project should be at least weekly.

Communication Barriers

The communication barriers between the editor and the president are typical in many organizations. Although the editor was responsible for writing about the merger, she could not get the necessary information from the company president. In this case, the project manager needs to help open up channels of communication and get the needed access to the president. This access may have been blocked by organizational culture or formal lines of communication.

Conflict Resolution

The project manager also needs to help resolve the conflict between the editor and designer on the layout of the report. The most effective strategy would be to facilitate a rational, problem-solving meeting where the editor and designer discuss their concerns, look at alternatives, and select the best approach. It may involve compromising on some issues. The project manager could help maintain a friendly atmosphere by emphasizing common areas of agreement. Getting more input from the company president may also help both parties better understand the intent of the report.

CHAPTER 30

Case Study: Chip Technologies

This case illustrates typical power struggles in project management between upper management, project managers, functional managers, and project team members.

Jan, the project manager was doomed from the beginning because Dan, the vice president, wanted control of the project and usurped her authority. Jan also didn't have the support of

Bob, the functional manager over engineering. Then, in an attempt to gain control, she used inappropriate methods to try to gain power.

To resolve these issues, all parties need to have an in-depth discussion about their roles and responsibilities and come to a consensus on how they will work together. Such a discussion may have to be mediated by the company president or an independent third party. Training on the types of power (influence, negotiation, and coercion) and the sources of power (expert, authority, reward, etc.) may help all parties appreciate each other's needs and understand better how to work together.

Jan may wish to try to gain expert power by showing Dan and Bob that she has the expertise to manage the project. Her power will also increase as she builds a better relationship with them. She can increase her referent power by finding ways to appropriately involve Dan in the project. If these approaches fail, she could approach the president and ask for formal authority to force Dan out of the project and require Bob to give her the resources she needs. This should be a last resort, because it would alienate key people who she should have on her side.

GLOSSARY

Activity. A unit of work performed during a project. An activity usually has a duration, a cost, and resource requirements. Also called task.

Activity estimate sheet. A form used to gather information needed to estimate a project activity.

Activity-on-arrow. A diagraming method that shows the activities on arrows, which are connected at nodes (circles) to show the dependencies. Also called arrow diagrams.

Activity-on-node. A diagraming method that shows the activities in a node (box) with arrows showing the dependencies. Also called precedence diagraming method.

Actual Cost (AC). The cost incurred to complete the work that was actually performed in a given time period. Also called actual cost of work performed (ACWP).

Alternative course of action review. A review to identify other things that could be done to solve the problem or take advantage of the opportunity instead of the approach being taken by the proposed project.

Analogy estimate. A method of estimating that uses the actual costs and durations of previous, similar projects as the basis for estimating the current project. Also called top-down estimating.

Arrow diagram. A diagram that shows the activities on arrows, which are connected at nodes (circles) to show the dependencies. Also called activity-on-arrow.

Baseline. The original schedule or cost plan for the project, including approved changes. This is the basis from which actual performance is measured to determine variances.

Bottom-up estimate. A method of estimating that sums the cost and duration of the individual work packages.

Budget at Completion (BAC). The estimated total cost of the project when completed.

Budgeted Cost of Work Performed (BCWP). See Earned value (EV).

Budgeted Cost of Work Scheduled (BCWS). See Planned value (PV).

Budgeting. The process of allocating the cost estimates to work items to establish a cost baseline for measuring project performance.

Cause-and-effect diagram. A graphical representation of the relationships that exist between factors. Used to explore a wide variety of factors and their relationships to factors that may cause them. Also called a fish bone diagram.

Change control. A formal process to manage proposed changes to the project plan. Includes processes for submitting, evaluating, approving, and communicating changes. Sometimes called configuration management.

Client. The person or group that requests a project.

Communication plan. A description of what information is communicated, to whom, how, and how often.

Conceptual review. A review to determine if the project fits within the organization's goals and if the project will solve the stated problem or appropriately take advantage of the current opportunity.

Configuration management. See Change control.

Contingency plan. A plan that describes the actions to be taken if a risk event should occur.

Contingency reserve. See Reserve.

Contract, cost-plus. See Cost-plus contract.

Contract, cost-reimbursable. See Cost-plus contract.

Contract, firm-fixed-price. See Fixed-price contract.

Contract, fixed-price. See Fixed-price contract.

Contract, time-and-materials. See Cost-plus contract.

Contract incentives. Additional payments included in contract terms, such as completing work before a given date or controlling costs to a given level.

Control charts. Graphs that display periodic results along with established control limits. They are used to determine if a process is in control or in need of adjustment.

Cost. The money and resources required to complete a project.

Cost budgeting. See Budgeting.

Cost control. The process of comparing actual expenditures to the baseline cost plans to determine variances, evaluate possible alternatives, and take the appropriate action.

Cost Performance Index (CPI). A ratio that measures cost efficiency by comparing budgeted costs to actual costs. In earned value analysis, the budgeted cost of work performed divided by the actual cost of work performed.

Cost-plus contract. A contract where the vendor agrees to do the work for the cost of time and materials, plus an agreed amount of profit. Also called cost-plus-fixed-fee, cost-reimbursable, or time-and-materials contract.

Cost-reimbursable contract. See Cost-plus contract.

Cost Variance (CV). The difference between the planned and actual cost of an activity. In earned value analysis, the difference between the budgeted cost of work performed and the actual cost of work performed.

CPM. See Critical path method.

Crashing the schedule. Taking action to decrease the total project duration after analyzing the options to determine how to get the maximum compression for the least cost.

Critical activity. An activity on the critical path.

Critical path. The path through the network that takes the longest total time, and therefore determines the earliest possible time the project can be completed. All activities on this path generally have zero float, meaning that the early and late start (and early and late finish) are the same.

Critical Path Method (CPM). A technique used to estimate project duration. It analyzes which sequence of activities (which path) has the least amount of scheduling flexibility (the least amount of float).

Customer. A person or group that will use the result of the project (the product, service, process, or plan).

Deliverable. Something delivered at the end of a project, such as a product, service, process, or plan.

Duration. The number of work periods (such as hours, days, or weeks) required to complete an activity. Does not include holidays or other non-working periods. Not the same as effort.

Early finish. The earliest date an activity can end.

Early start. The earliest date an activity can begin.

Earned Value (EV). The planned cost of work actually performed in a given time period. Also called budgeted cost of work performed (BCWP).

Earned value analysis. A method of measuring and evaluating project performance. It compares the amount of work planned with what is actually accomplished to determine if the project is on track. Earned value analysis is also known as variance analysis.

Effort. The number of labor units required to complete an activity. Also called work effort. Not the same as duration.

Enterprise portfolio management. Managing all projects of the organization as a whole by setting priorities and allocating resources across projects.

Estimate at Completion (EAC). The expected total cost of the project when completed, including adjustments to the original estimate based on project performance to date. In earned value analysis, AC + ETC.

Estimate to Complete (ETC). The expected additional cost needed to complete the project, including adjustments to the original estimate based on project performance to date. In earned value analysis, (BAC − EV) / CPI.

Exception report. A report that shows only major deviations from the project plan, rather than all deviations.

Fast tracking. Compressing the project schedule by changing the sequence of activities to allow activities to be done in parallel (at the same time) or to allow some to overlap.

Feasibility study. A review to determine if the project can realistically be accomplished.

Finish-to-finish activity relationship. A dependency between activities where one activity must finish before the other can finish.

Finish-to-start activity relationship. A dependency between activities where one activity must finish before the other can begin.

Firm-fixed-price contract. See Fixed-price contract.

Fish bone diagram. See Cause-and-effect diagram.

Fixed-price contract. A contract where the vendor agrees to do the total work for a fixed price. Also called firm-fixed-price contract or lump-sum contract.

Float. The time an activity can slip without delaying the project finish date. It is equal to the difference between the early start and late start (or the difference between the early finish and late finish). Also known as slack, total float, and path float. See also Free float.

Flowchart. A quality control tool that provides information about process flow.

Free float. The amount of time an activity can slip without delaying the early start of any activity that immediately follows it. See also Float.

Functional manager. A person assigned to manage a specific function (such as accounting, manufacturing, or marketing) and provide technical direction. Also called resource manager.

Functional organization. A hierarchical organizational structure where each functional division has its own project managers who operate independently from project managers in other divisions.

Gantt chart. A bar chart of schedule information, typically with dates across the horizontal axis, activities listed down the vertical axis, and activity durations shown as horizontal bars under the appropriate dates.

Incentives. See Contract incentives.

Integration management. The processes required to ensure that the various elements of the project are properly coordinated.

Internal rate of return. A profitability measure that represents an average rate of return for the project, expressed as a percentage.

Lag. The time delay between the start or finish of one activity and the start or finish of another activity. When expressed as a negative number, lag indicates an overlap in the activities and is also called lead.

Late finish. The latest date an activity can end and still allow the project to be completed on time.

Late start. The latest date an activity can begin and still allow the project to be completed on time.

Lead. The time overlap between the start or finish of one activity and the start or finish of another activity. See also Lag.

Logic network diagram. See Network diagram.

Lump-sum contract. See Fixed-price contract.

Management reserves. See Reserves.

Matrix organizational structure. An organizational structure which is a blend of functional and project structures. The project team reports both to a project manager (who provides project management skills) and to a functional manager (who provides specific job-related skills).

Milestone. A point in time that marks the start or finish of a significant activity or group of activities, usually the completion of a major deliverable. A milestone has no duration, cost, or resource requirements.

Milestone schedule. A schedule that includes only significant (milestone) activities. Also called a summary schedule.

Mitigation plans. Steps taken to lower the probability of the risk event happening or reduce the impact should it occur.

Network diagram. A graphical flow plan of the activities that must be accomplished to complete the project. It shows the planned sequence of steps, time requirements, interdependencies, and interrelationships. Also called precedence diagram.

Objectives. The statement of cost, time, and scope required to complete a project.

Opportunity cost. The cost of choosing one alternative (project) and, therefore, giving up the potential benefits of another alternative (project).

Parallel activities. Two or more activities that occur at the same time. Also called concurrent or simultaneous activities.

Parametric estimate. A method of estimating that uses mathematical parameters (such as a dollar amount per square foot) to predict project costs.

Pareto diagram. A bar chart with elements arranged in descending order of importance, generally by magnitude of frequency, cost, or time. Used to focus attention on the most critical issues.

Pareto Principle. A vital few elements (20 percent) account for the majority (80 percent) of the problems.

Path float. See Float.

Payback period. The number of periods (usually years) until cumulative revenues exceed cumulative costs, and therefore, the project has "turned a profit."

Percent complete. A method of reporting where the amount of work completed on an activity is expressed as a percent of the total work required for the activity.

Performance management. The ongoing process of minimizing the number and impact of problems and providing an environment wherein the project can succeed.

PERT. See Program Evaluation and Review Technique.

Planned Value (PV). The planned cost of work scheduled to be done in a given time period. Also called budgeted cost of work scheduled (BCWS).

Portfolio management. Managing all projects of the organization as a portfolio.

Precedence diagram. See Network diagram.

Precedence diagraming method (PDM). A network diagraming method that shows the activities in a node (box) with arrows showing the dependencies. Also called activity-on-node.

Predecessor activity. An activity that occurs before another activity in a project.

Preliminary risk review. An initial review of the potential risks involved in a project to determine if the expected benefits of the project are worth the risk.

Program Evaluation and Review Technique (PERT). A technique used to estimate project duration. It uses the critical path method and a weighted average of estimates for each activity.

Project. "A temporary endeavor undertaken to create a unique product or service." A project has a definite beginning and end. (See PMI, *A Guide to the Project Management Body of Knowledge*, 2000, p. 4.)

Project charter. A set of documents that states the purpose and requirements of the project, including approvals by the client or senior management and the authority of the project manager to expend resources.

Project closure. Formal steps taken at the conclusion of a project to get acceptance of the final product, close project records, and reallocate personnel and other resources.

Project management. A set of principles, methods, and techniques used to plan and control project work effectively.

Project manager. The person who manages a specific project, who is expected to meet the approved objectives of the project, including project scope, budget, and schedule.

Project objectives. See Objectives.

Project organization. An organizational structure in which an autonomous division of project managers is responsible for planning, controlling, managing, and reporting the progress of all projects in the organization.

Quality assurance. The process of evaluating project performance to ensure compliance with quality standards.

Reserves. Provisions in the project plan to mitigate the impact of risk events. Usually in the form of contingency reserves (funds to cover unplanned costs), schedule reserves (extra time to apply to schedule overruns), or management reserves (funds held by general management to apply to projects that overrun).

Resource. Funds, personnel, equipment, facilities, or materials needed to complete an activity or a project.

Resource control. The process of comparing actual performance to the resource plans to determine variances, evaluate possible alternatives, and take the appropriate action.

Resource histogram. A chart showing the commitment of resources over a period of time.

Resource leveling. Taking action to minimize the peaks when resources are over allocated.

Resource manager. See Functional manager.

Responsibility Assignment Matrix. A chart that relates skill requirements to people (or groups of people).

Return on assets. A measure of net profit divided by total assets.

Return on investment. A measure of net profit divided by total investment.

Return on sales. A measure of net profit divided by total sales.

Risk management. The process of identifying possible risks, making preventive and contingency plans, and executing those plans when risk events occur.

Risk management plan. A plan that documents the procedures that will be used to manage risk throughout the project.

Risk review, preliminary. See Preliminary risk review.

Rolling wave estimate. A method of estimating that provides a gross estimate for the entire project and periodically calculates detailed estimates for the next short period of time.

Schedule Performance Index (SPI). A ratio that measures schedule efficiency by comparing work performed to work scheduled. In earned value analysis, the budgeted cost of work performed divided by the budgeted cost of work scheduled.

Schedule reserves. See Reserves.

Schedule Variance (SV). The difference between the scheduled and actual completion of an activity. In earned value analysis, the difference between the budgeted cost of work scheduled and the budgeted cost of work performed.

Scope. A description of the features and functions of the end products or services to be provided by the project.

Scope control. The process of comparing actual performance to the scope statement to determine variances, evaluate possible alternatives, and take the appropriate action.

Scope creep. The tendency for scope to increase during the course of the project without proportionate increases in time or cost.

Scope statement. A narrative description of the project objectives, including justification for the project, description of the product or service to be created, and a list of the project deliverables.

Scope verification. Verifying that all project deliverables have been accomplished as agreed.

Sequential activities. Two or more activities that occur one after the other. Also called consecutive activities.

Simulation estimate. A method of estimating that calculates multiple costs or durations with different sets of assumptions.

Slack. See Float.

Stakeholders. People who are affected by or have an interest in the project, including clients, senior management, middle management, functional managers, project managers, project team members, customers, and vendors.

Start-to-finish activity relationship. A dependency between activities where one activity must begin before the other can finish.

Start-to-start activity relationship. A dependency between activities where one activity must begin before the other can begin.

Statement of work. A narrative description of the work to be accomplished. A general statement of work may apply to the entire project while a more specific statement of work may apply to a project activity or the work of an individual team member.

Successor activity. An activity that occurs after another activity in a project.

Summary schedule. A schedule that includes only significant (milestone) activities. Also called a milestone schedule.

Task. See Activity.

Team members. The people who work with the project manager directly or indirectly to accomplish project goals and complete project activities.

Time. The time required to complete a project.

Time-and-materials contract. See Cost-plus contract.

Time control. The process of comparing actual schedule performance to the baseline schedule to determine variances, evaluate possible alternatives, and take the appropriate action.

Total float. See Float.

Trend analysis. Using mathematical techniques to forecast future outcomes based on historical results.

Trigger. An occurrence or condition that causes an event to happen.

Unit-price contract. A contract where the vendor agrees to a preset amount per unit of service (for example, $90 per hour).

Work breakdown structure. A hierarchical breakdown of activities and end products which organizes and defines all work to be completed in a project.

Work effort. The number of labor units required to complete an activity. Also called effort. Not the same as duration.

Work packages. The deliverables in the lowest level of the work breakdown structure. A work package may be divided into the specific activities to be performed.

Workaround. The response to an unplanned risk event.

❖❖❖
APPENDIX C

SUGGESTED READINGS AND RESOURCES

READINGS

James P. Lewis. *Fundamentals of Project Management*. New York: AMACOM, 1997.

The Project Management Institute. *A Guide to the Project Management Body of Knowledge* (PMBOK Guide). Upper Darby, Pa: PMI, 2000.

Harold Kerzner. *Project Management: A Systems Approach to Planning, Scheduling, and Controlling, 7th edition*. New York: John Wiley & Sons, 2001.

Harold Kerzner. *In Search of Excellence in Project Management*. New York: Van Nostrand Reinhold, 1998.

J. Davidson Frame. *The New Project Management*. San Francisco: Jossey-Bass, 1994.

David I. Cleland and William R. King. *Project Management Handbook*. New York: Van Nostrand Reinhold, 1983.

Jack R. Meredith and Samuel J. Mantel, Jr. *Project Management: A Managerial Approach*. New York: John Wiley & Sons, 1995.

RESOURCES

Project Management Institute (PMI) (Four Campus Blvd., Newton Square, PA 19073, phone: 610-356-4600, *www.pmi.org*) establishes project management standards, provides seminars, educational programs and the PMP® professional certification. Founded in 1969, this professional organization has over 70,000 members worldwide.

International Project Management Association, P.O. Box 30, Monmouth NP25 4YZ, United Kingdom, phone: +44 1594 531007, fax: +44 1594 531008, *www.ipma.ch*, admin@ipma. freeserve.co.uk. IPMA is a nonprofit organization founded in 1965 that promotes project management internationally through its membership network of project management associations, individuals, and companies. It provides certification, conferences, seminars, courses, research, and publications.

American Management Association, 1601 Broadway, New York, NY 10019, phone: 800-262-9699, *www.amanet.org*. AMA offers courses on project management. AMA's publishing arm, AMACOM, is one of the world's largest publishers of books on project management.

George Washington University, in association with Educational Services Institute (2100 Pennsylvania Ave., N.W., Suite 250, Washington, D.C. 20037-3202, phone: 202-994-7375, *www.esi-intl.com*) offers classes, including masters and doctorate degrees in project management.

University of Phoenix (phone: 800-228-7240, *www.phoenix.edu*) has campuses in more than fifteen states, and offers classes, including a bachelor of science degree in project management.

ProjectWorld events (*www.ProjectWorld.com*, phone: 888-827-6699) combine a practical education in project management with a world-class exposition hall to meet the needs of today's project and business professionals.

WEB SITES

Need help solving a project problem? Searching for an online forum or information exchange? The following portals bring a community of project managers and information right to your fingertips.

www.pmi.org
www.ipma.org
www.ProjectConnections.com
www.projectmanagement.com
www.project-manager.com
www.pmforum.org
www.pmboulevard.com
www.gantthead.com
www.ipma.ch
www.projectman.org

The purchase of this book grants you access to a special Internet site with additional project management information. Log on to the Project Management Center at *www.projectman.org* and access special areas of the site using the password *projectboy*.

INDEX